THE LIBRARY
ST. MARY'S COLLEGE OF MARYLAND
ST. MARY'S CITY, MARYLAND 20686

74521

TWAYNE'S WORLD AUTHORS SERIES

A Survey of the World's Literature

Sylvia E. Bowman, Indiana University

GENERAL EDITOR

SPAIN

Janet Winecoff Díaz
University of North Carolina at Chapel Hill

Gerald E. Wade
Vanderbilt University

EDITORS

Ramón Gómez de la Serna

TWAS 338

Ramón Gómez de la Serna

Ramón Gómez de la Serna

By RITA (MAZZETTI) GARDIOL
Ball State University

Twayne Publishers, Inc. :: New York

Copyright © 1974 by Twayne Publishers, Inc.

All Rights Reserved

Library of Congress Cataloging in Publication Data

Gardiol, Rita Mazzetti.
  Ramón Gómez de la Serna.

(Twayne's world authors series, TWAS 338)
Bibliography: p. 159.
1. Gómez de la Serna, Ramón, 1888-1963.
PQ6613.04Z726   868'.6'209 [B]   74-13340
ISBN 0-8057-2379-X

MANUFACTURED IN THE UNITED STATES OF AMERICA

To René

Contents

    About the Author
    Preface
    Chronology
1. Literary Life   15
2. Fiction: Articles, Essays, Drama, Pantomimes   36
3. Fiction: Novels   42
4. Fiction: Novelettes, "Superhistorical" Novels, Short Stories   62
5. Biography   99
6. Unpublished Works   121
7. Style: Ramón's Expressive System   126
8. Conclusion   145
    Notes and References   147
    Selected Bibliography   159
    Index   171

About the Author

Rita Gardiol is an Associate Professor of Spanish at Ball State University, Muncie, Indiana where she has served as Coordinator of Spanish, and is currently Spanish Graduate Advisor and Administrative Assistant in the Department of Foreign Languages. She has taught at Mt. Mercy College in Pittsburgh, Pennsylvania and was a teaching fellow at the University of Indiana, Bloomington, Indiana.

Dr. Gardiol graduated from Mt. Mercy College with honor, received fellowships for study at Middlebury College, Vermont, where she was granted her Master's degree, and at Indiana University where she completed her Ph.D. In addition she has studied at the Catholic University in Ponce, Puerto Rico, at the University for Foreigners in Perugia, Italy, and was a Fulbright Scholar at the University of Madrid in 1963-64. Her articles have appeared in *Hispania, Hispanófila, Kentucky Romance Quarterly, Romance Notes,* the *Language Quarterly* and other scholarly journals.

Preface

In writing about Ramón Gómez de la Serna, the sheer volume of his literary output makes coherent and logical organization as essential as it is difficult. The organization used here is arbitrary in the sense that it is often not chronological but thematič. For compression, novel-length essay-type works are discussed in conjunction with Ramón's literary development since they reflect his interests and preoccupations at different life periods. His individually published essays, so numerous and disperse as to make their collection quite difficult, are given only minor attention. His dramas and pantomimes, difficult to obtain, rarely performed, and largely ignored by critics, are treated succinctly to save necessary space for the stories and biographical studies which form the major portion of his literary output. The division used here of "fictional" and "biographical" works is perhaps misleading, since Ramón always wrote with creative imagination. Yet, because biography is a distinct genre and his prolific biographical studies include some of his best and least known work, they deserve special consideration. Since style is paramount in Ramón, his *greguerías* and other stylistic devices are examined separately in a final chapter, although stress has been placed throughout this book on his innovative and artistic use of imagery and other basically poetic qualities.

It is the writer's hope that this study will reveal much of the verbal, visual, and creative magic which characterized Ramón Gómez de la Serna and will stimulate an increased interest in his work.

Acknowledgments are due to Professor Miguel Enguídanos for stimulating my interest in Ramón, to Professor Eldon Jenkins for proofreading the manuscript, and to Iris Ridgeway for typing it.

Chronology

1888 July 3: Born in Madrid (Spain).
1904 Mother died.
1905 Published first book, *Entrando en fuego (Going Under Fire)*.
1906 Met Carmen de Burgos. Began liaison and lifelong friendship.
1909- Paris sojourn. Worked at political post obtained for him by
1911 his father.
1911 Began writing for *La Tribuna*, Madrid daily newspaper; invented the *greguería*. Began occasional use of penname, "Tristán."
1914 Published *El doctor inverosímil (The Unlikely Doctor)*.
1915 Established his first independent apartment. Publication of *El rastro (The Flea Market)*.
1917 Published *La viuda blanca y negra (The Black and White Widow)*, *El circo (The Circus)*, *Senos, (Bosoms)*, *Greguerías*. Began Pombo *tertulia*.
1918 *Pombo*, Volume I, *Muestrarios (Samplings)*, *El alba (The Dawn)* published. Began regular column in Madrid newspaper, *El liberal*.
1920 Publication of *Variaciones (Variations)*, *Virguerías (Virginal Glimpses)*, *Libro nuevo (New Book)*.
1921 Publishes *Disparates (Absurdities)*.
1922 Ramón's father died. *El incongruente (The Incongruent One)*, *El secreto del acueducto (The Secret of the Aqueduct)*, *El gran hotel (Grand Hotel)* published.
1923 Began to write for *El Sol*, Madrid; moved to *torreón* apartment. Began construction of "El Ventanal," dream home in Estoril, Portugal. Accepted Ortega's offer to write for the newly founded *Revista de Occidente*. Published *Ramonismo (Ramonism)*, *La quinta de Palmyra (Palmyra's Country Villa)*, *Cinelandia (Movieland)*, *El novelista (The Novelist)*, *El chalet de las rosas (The Chalet of the Roses)*.

1924 *La sagrada cripta del Pombo (Pombo, The Sacred Crypt)*, Vol. II published.
1925 Publishes *Caprichos (Caprices)*.
1926 Publication of *Gollerías (Tidbits)*. Forced to sell "El Ventanal." In financial straits, fled to Naples. Wrote and published *El torero Caracho (Caracho, the Toreador)*.
1927 Publishes *La mujer de ámbar (The Amber Woman)*.
1928 Began writing paying column in *La Nación* newspaper, Buenos Aires. Published *El caballero del hongo gris (The Gentleman in the Grey Top Hat), Goya*.
1929 Publication of *Efigies (Effigies)*, a collection of his biographical prologues. Attempted theater — *Los medios seres (The Half-Beings)*. It failed. Undertook lecture series in Berlin.
1930 Broadcast series of late-night radio chats from his study. Published *La Nardo (The Spikenard), Azorín*.
1931 Left *El Sol* for political reasons. Advent of the Republic. Gave a lecture series in Buenos Aires. Met Russian Jewish divorcee, Luisa Sofovich, who later became his wife. Published *Ismos (Isms)*.
1932 Gave lecture tour of Spanish provinces accompanied by Luisa. Published *Policéfalo y señora (Polycephalous and Wife)*.
1933 Second lecture series in Buenos Aires. After return to Madrid, Luisa critically ill. Wrote *El Greco*.
1935 Revised *Los muertos y las muertas (Dead Men and Dead Women)*, written in 1922, and published it together with *Otras fantasmagorías (Other Phantasmagories)*.
1936 Fled to Buenos Aires to escape impending Spanish Civil War. Published *¡Rebeca!*.
1941 Publication of *Retratos contemporáneos (Contemporary Portraits)*.
1942 Publishes *Mi tía Carolina Coronado (My Aunt, Carolina Coronado)*.
1944 Began writing for *Arriba*, Madrid pro-Franco newspaper. Published *José Gutiérrez Solana, Don Ramón María del Valle-Inclán, Doña Juana la loca (Doña Juana the Mad)*.
1945 Publishes *Lope de Vega. Nuevos retratos contemporáneos (New Contemporary Portraits)*.
1947 Publication of *El hombre perdido (The Lost Man), Trampantojos (Tricks of Whimsy), Obras selectas (Selected Works)*.
1948 Publishes *Automoribundia (Autodeathography)*.

Chronology

- 1949 Visit to Madrid. Publication of *Cartas a las golondrinas (Letters to the Swallows), Las tres gracias (The Three Graces).*
- 1953 *Quevedo, Edgar Poe, el genio de América (Edgar Poe, the Genius of America)* published.
- 1954 Fiftieth anniversary of literary career. Publication of *Lope viviente (The Living Lope).* Contracted for *Obras completas (Complete Works).*
- 1955 Suffered repercussions from Perón's downfall in Argentina, lost articles, columns, pay.
- 1956 *Nostalgias de Madrid (Nostalgias of Madrid), Cartas a mí miso (Letters to Myself), Obras completas (Complete Works), Vol. I* published.
- 1957 Publication of *Obras completas (Complete Works) Vol. II, Nuevas páginas de mi vida (New Pages of My Life).*
- 1959 Publishes *Biografías completas (Complete Biographies).*
- 1960 Received Juan Paloma Award for literature.
- 1961 Publication of *Piso bajo (Basement Flat), Retratos completos (Complete Portraits).*
- 1962 January 31: received "special" March Award; other awards from Galicia, Catalonia. April 9: received official March Award.
- 1963 January 12: died. Transported to Madrid, buried in Panteón de Hombres Ilustres.

CHAPTER 1

Ramón's Literary Life

I *The First Years*

RAMÓN Gómez de la Serna's life was inextricably interwoven with his writing. Some of the factors which proved most significant in forming his particular sensibility and style as an artist were his freshness of vision and almost magical powers of imagination and association, his appreciation of plastic art forms and his unique sense of humor. These were developed during his early childhood in Madrid. Other qualities, like his intransigent and uncompromising literary ideals, were developed in the bohemian years of his adolescence and young manhood in the Spanish capital and in Paris; still other elements, no less essential in shaping his overall perspective of life evolved in the long struggle with poverty, loneliness, and the virtual abandonment by others that marked his maturer and declining years in Argentina.

Only the highlights of Gómez de la Serna's life will be considered here, and then always in relation to his literary output. It is almost impossible to consider them in any other way, for, in the fifty-nine years of his practice of literature (from the appearance of his first book in 1905 when he was sixteen, until his death in 1963 at the age of seventy-five) every major aspect of his existence was reflected in his writing.

Ramón seemed fully aware of the childhood experiences which had engendered his unusual powers of perception, imagination, and association, and took pains to record them in his autobiography. He tells us, for example,[1] that when he was in grammar school, two girl cousins, confined to a convent boarding school except for one day's liberty each year, customarily spent that day with his family. Seeing the wonder and delight they derived from observing the simple things so commonplace to him, Ramón learned a lesson he never forgot. Eager for similar piquant experiences, he made a game of seeing things with the same sense of newness as they. The practice became a lifetime habit, for he taught himself thenceforth to approach not only things, but even concepts and words as though he had never seen or heard of them before. The result was so different an approach to reality that when it is encountered in his work, it both surprises and delights the reader.

Another factor which played a role in the development of Ramón's imaginative powers was — almost incredibly — the outhouse at his grandmother's home. In his autobiography, Ramón recalls how, as a child, having been sent to his grandmother's for an extended visit while his brothers and sister had whooping cough, he frequently hid there to escape her constant vigilance. Writing of it in his adult years, he described it clearly: "she had pasted pictures there . . . the cubicle was completely covered . . . it touched off the imagination . . . there I learned my fondness for covering walls.[2]

Realizing the valuable evocative powers of this wallpaper-like conglomeration of pictures, Ramón utilized this discovery all his life by adorning the walls of his study with similar arrays of chaotically arranged pictures whose object was to stimulate his imagination by suggesting new and different associations. These techniques resulted in novel associations such as:

The rainbow is the scarf of the sky.[3]

Capital B is the nursemaid of the alphabet.[4]

The interest in art which eventually brought Ramón to write biographical studies of some of Spain's most important painters — El Greco, Velázquez, Goya, Solana, Picasso, Dalí, and a host of others — also had its beginnings in his childhood when he frequently spent Sunday afternoons in the Prado Museum with his father. The habit of making such excursions to the Prado was one that he continued to cultivate all his life. It helped him to acquire an acute consciousness of the creative similarities between the artist and the writer. In all the biographies of artists that Gómez de la Serna wrote throughout his lifetime, he continued to manifest this deep awareness of the relationship between art and literature.

The humorous mode of expression that was to become almost a hallmark of Gómez de la Serna's style may have had its beginning in his formative years, when it was largely occasioned by his adolescent desire to live up to the title "humorist" which an uncle had conferred

Literary Life

on him one day when he found his wit amusing. Ramón later indicated in his autobiography how deliberately he had striven to live up to the title. The humor he developed had a special quality about it which his cousin Gaspar, writing about him later, described as "a kind . . . of happy hypothetical reality; transfiguring reality."[5]

Many years later, in an essay entitled, significantly, "Gravedad e importancia del humorismo" ("Gravity and Importance of Humor"), Ramón discussed the concept of humor that he had gradually evolved, carefully distinguishing it from irony, cynicism, sarcasm, mockery, the grotesque, the burlesque, the clownish, and the ridiculous. For him, earlier than for other vanguardists, humor came to be "the surest approach to the ephemeral quality of life."[6]

II *The Beginnings of Ramón's Literary Career*

Discounting the schoolboy publication of a home-printed newssheet, it may be said that Ramón's literary career began in 1905 when his indulgent father financed the publication of his first book: *Entrando en fuego (Going Under Fire)*. The moral and financial support which the young writer continued to receive from his father freed him from economic need and enabled him to develop a uniqueness of style and freedom of expression which he earnestly cherished thereafter. Paternal support did more: when the aspiring young writer completed his *bachillerato,* his father gave him a trip to Paris; when he completed his *licenciatura,* his father founded *Prometeo,* a literary magazine, and made the young man editor. It was a position which gave Ramón opportunities of inestimable value, providing him a means of publishing his works and an avenue of introduction to other writers. In soliciting contributions, Ramón made valuable literary acquaintances as he corresponded with authors of established reputation like Juan Ramón Jiménez and Gabriel Miró.

In 1908, the elder Gómez de la Serna's repeated attempts to obtain a political post in Paris for his son were successful and the optimistic young author returned there for a prolonged stay. He could hardly have gone to Paris at a more stimulating time; everything was happening at once. Proust, Apollinaire, Larbaud, Colette, Gide — all were writing, and Shattuck, describing the vitality of this period which lasted until World War I, says: "It is almost as if the war had to come in order to put an end to an extravaganza that could not have sustained itself at this level."[7] The young writer immersed himself in Paris, absorbing its multitudinous sights, sounds, and smells. Daybreak in Paris fascinated him, and, with the "patience of a poet and the fervor of a lover,"[8] he captured his impressions of it in a book called simply *El alba. (The Dawn).*

The streets where Nerval had wandered on the night of his suicide, the Luxembourg Gardens where Remy de Gourmont had been inspired to write *Une nuit au Luxembourg,* the cafes where his literary idols had gathered — everything in Paris exhilarated Ramón and he described his sensations saying: "I felt myself a liberal in the asylum of that Paris of 1909," "I lent myself to all the experiences that were transforming but not degrading," "I had gone to Paris to enlarge the mysterious destiny of my soul, to communicate with street lamps, to find an incomparable partner, to dine in different restaurants every day until I got to a hundred thousand. When they call me by name, I ought not to answer. I am another. Another who is myself, more myself than myself."[9]

III   Return to Madrid

After two years in Paris, Ramón lost his post because of political changes at home. His return to Madrid was fortunate: shortly after his arrival, he was invited to write for *La Tribuna,* a daily newspaper of considerable circulation. Although the prospect offered no remuneration, he grasped it in the hope that it would indeed serve him as a "tribune" from which to reach a larger public. His one goal now was to be a writer and when Prime Minister Canalejas, as a gesture of friendship for his father, offered him a position as his private secretary, the young writer refused. Later, however, his more practical father insisted he accept a political post proffered by García Prieto. Although Ramón accepted the position, he soon relinquished it saying it made him feel "like a prisoner."[10] Throughout his life, Ramón continued to refuse the political or teaching positions offered him, remaining steadfastly determined to earn his living by his pen.

It was in the first year after his return to Madrid that perhaps the most felicitous moment in the young writer's life took place. One summer morning, looking out from his balcony in Madrid, he recalled a similar, cooler morning when, on his first visit to Italy, he had looked down on the Arno River from his balcony in Florence. Quite possibly he wished himself back there, when the thought occurred to him that perhaps the river too might like to move! Perhaps, for example, the far bank longed to exchange places with the near one![11] Delighted with the unorthodoxy of his concept, Ramón contrived other similar ones until they were swarming in his mind. He sought a name by which to label these novel concepts and identify them as uniquely his own. A word occurred to him whose meaning he immediately sought in the dictionary: "Greguería, outbreak, confused outcry."[12] He decided to make the word his own. With his discovery of the *greguería*, Ramón had found the inimitable mode of expression that was to be the salient aspect of his style.

The young man's intense desire to live a purely literary life soon caused him to cultivate only friendships compatible with his literary ideal. When at twenty he met the handsome, amply-proportioned Carmen de Burgos, ten years older than he and an established author in her own right, he effected an ingenious liaison of love and literature. Carmen nurtured his dedication to literature, and they spent long hours together, writing, reading, correcting, criticizing, and sharing their works.[13] Quite possibly Ramón (whose mother had died two years earlier) sought in Carmen's mature devotion a love that was not only sentimental and intellectual, but somewhat maternal as well. It was Carmen who first interested him in biographical writing by asking him to compose a biographical prologue on Ruskin to accompany her translation of the writer's *Stones of Venice*. Later, when Ramón wrote other biographical studies, she aided him by gathering and organizing data.[14]

In 1915, Ramón moved away from home so that he could spend more time with Carmen and devote more time to writing. He tried his hand at producing a full-length novel, and, in 1917, brought forth *La viuda blanca y negra (The Black and White Widow)*, a novel about a woman who passed as a widow so that she might seek consolation with her gullible suitor.

El circo (The Circus) and *Senos (Bosoms)* followed that same year along with a volume of *Greguerías*. *The Circus* and *Bosoms* were not novels, but works of an indeterminate genre that might be called "works of accumulation." In them, Ramón assembled a number of verbal sketches (not quite stories) with long enumerations of visual or tactile images. In *The Circus*, with typical vanguardist exuberance, he presents the trapeze artists, tight-rope walkers, clowns, bicyclists, elephants, and those elements that form part of the colorful thrill and excitement of the spectacle. *Bosoms*, as the title indicates, is a book entirely about bosoms, in which the author takes ingenious delight in literally cataloguing bosoms of all sizes, shapes, and kinds. There are chapters entitled, "An Oriental Bosom Vendor," "Bosoms in Art," "Andalusian Bosoms," and so forth, all cleverly and whimsically skirting the pornographic or offensive. Ramón was experimenting with all forms of expression. Cardona has noted that *Bosoms* was the book of tactile sensations, *The Circus* the book of visual sensations, and *Greguerías* the book of the imagination."[15]

Other writers besides Carmen made a lasting impression on the young author. Silverio Lanza (Juan Bautista Amorós), for example, whom Ramón met in 1909, with his philosophical approach to social reform, originality and sobriety of literary expression, seemed, to Gómez de la Serna and the young men of his generation, a true successor to Larra. They admired his aesthetic liberty, humor, enormous independence, and colorful personality. When Lanza died, Ramón considered it both a duty and an honor to collect his unpublished papers for a posthumous work called *Páginas escogidas e inéditas de Silverio Lanza (Selected and Unpublished Pages of Silverio Lanza)*, which appeared in 1918. But of all the writers whom he met during this period, it was Azorín who became the object of Ramón's virtual hero worship.[16] Perhaps it was "the little philosopher's" love for *things,* savoring their every facet and exhausting their every possibility, that made the younger writer feel akin to him. In Ramón, this tendency is particularly evident in books like *Bosoms, The Circus* and *El rastro (The Flea Market).* In Azorín, it can be seen in works like *España, Un pueblecito* and *Doña Inés,* among others.

Whereas Azorín contents himself with merely enumerating and cataloguing commonplace things, Ramón goes further and imbues them with human qualities and histories. Both writers tend to develop their themes in a leisurely manner, and seem to delight more in revealing the details of their stories than in coming to the point of their narrations. While Ramón comments on Azorín's tendency to lengthen every scene,[17] Cardona observes that in reading Ramón, "the pleasure consists precisely of being there, not in getting anyplace."[18]

Ramón's boundless admiration for Madrid's literary and bohemian figures led him to habituate the cafes they frequented. Thus, he came to recognize the bohemian figure of Alejandro Sawa and to observe at firsthand the close friendship that existed between him and Valle-Inclán. Ramón believed that Valle identified with Sawa, and perceived that it was Sawa who imbued Valle with the idea that "there is something grand in pure poetic poverty."[19] Ramón's biography of Valle bears evidence of the warm personal affection he felt for him and of the deep respect which Valle's uncompromising dedication to literature inspired in him.

IV Pombo

Gómez de la Serna's warm personality and good nature helped him to make friends easily, and he soon developed a following among

Literary Life

the youthful writers of Madrid. When he felt the need of establishing his own *tertulia,* and sought a cafe suitable for a meeting place, Ramón found the Pombo, genteel in its old-fashioned way. The Pombo soon became his headquarters. There he met friends, exchanged ideas, read manuscripts, wrote novels, and even received mail. Solana eventually immortalized the Pombo *tertulia* in painting and Ramón did the same in writing. The Saturday night sessions at the Pombo were always lively. Writers and artists turned up there either in answer to Ramón's personal invitation or simply out of curiosity. As Ramón's popularity grew, so did Pombo's. It came to be *the* literary *tertulia* of the period. Men of letters visiting from abroad came to consider it a mark of distinction to be invited there. Among others came Latin America's Pedro Henríquez Ureña, Alfonso Reyes, Torres Bodet, González Martinez, Martín Luis Guzmán, Pablo Neruda, and Rómulo Gallegos; Germany's Karl Vossler; Switzerland's Tristán Tzara; Russia's Lipchitz; Italy's Giovanni Papini and D'Annunzio. Even professors from American universities such as William L. Fichter from Brown and F. Courtney Tarr from Princeton made their way to Pombo. The vitalizing force of these gatherings was, of course, Ramón, who, like a skilled director, achieved a rich blending of the unharmonious voices that rose to proclaim, protest, or defend the most unlikely variety of new and stimulating ideas.

In addition to the Pombo, one of Ramón's favorite places was Madrid's flea market, the Rastro. He was intrigued by its magnificent disorder and never walked through it without buying something to add to the Rastro-in-miniature that was his study. In addition to covering his walls with a fantastic array of pictures, Ramón had by now gone further and begun to surround himself with a chaotic collection of things: mechanical birds, toy soldiers, bottles and boxes, clocks and paperweights, ceramics and ornamental crystal balls, a discarded chimney, a tombstone, a street lamp, a life-size mannikin. Even the damaged and broken articles heaped in the Rastro intrigued Ramón. His imagination imbued them with life, and through it he tried to visualize their past. This absorption in the Rastro found expression in a book by that title. Dedicated, significantly, to Azorín, it was Ramón's first book to find a professional publisher and it revealed an emphasis on things wholly new to literature.

While most critics, because of this intense fascination which Ramón manifests for things, label him a realist, Julián Marías insists that, paradoxically, he really is not, and precisely because he goes beyond reality: "This passion for reality has saved Ramón from being a realist. The realist believes that things are no more than things; it is the 'REIST' who forgets the reality of things [and] goes beyond. ... "Never is Ramón more Ramón — and less a realist — than when he seems to enjoy, to take delight in, things."[20]

Marías notes that Ramón never speaks of "the" bottle, "the" streetlamp, of individual, unique things, but that he speaks rather in the plural, referring, for example, to "containers," "bottles," "flasks," or "pipes." To Marías, these enumerative plurals indicate Ramón's inebriation with things. He credits Ramón with multiple, rather than simple vision, noting that he looks at things, and looks again, then returns to look yet again, so enchanted by the things he sees that he cannot go on.

The Flea Market was disregarded by literary critics. Perhaps the book was simply ahead of its time. Ramón published it in 1915, and even in French literature the tendency to write about "things" as such did not become noteworthy until after 1930, and it increased in concentration and frequency after the Second World War.[21]

V *World War I and Its Aftermath*

The first jolting experience which Ramón and the optimistic young men of his generation experienced came with World War I. Although Spain did not participate in the war, its tremendous impact could not go unheeded. In the autumn of 1914, refugees like the Mexican painter Diego Rivera and the Russian sculptor Lipchitz came to Madrid from Paris, bringing with them a spirit of unrest and a desire for literary and artistic renovation. With this new influx of life, the *tertulia* of Pombo prospered and achieved even greater importance. *Pombo,* at once a biography of the cafe, a collection of biographical sketches of the men who frequented it, and an autobiographical chapter of Ramón's life, appeared in 1918.

When the end of the war came, a wave of optimism swept Spain and fresh ideas were heard and discussed eagerly in the cafes. Ramón, too, had reason to be optimistic, for finally, he achieved his goal of writing a paid column for a major publication, *El liberal.* It is an interesting commentary on his character that, much as he had desired such a position, Ramón hesitated to accept it until he was assured that it would not require him to abandon his unpaid articles for *La Tribuna.* His sense of indebtedness to the paper that had given him his start made him unwilling to abandon it even when offered remuneration elsewhere. Several years later, when Tomás Borrás, on behalf of *La Voz,* and Ortega, on behalf of *El Sol,* made him tempting offers of more than six times the salary he was being paid by *El liberal,* Ramón's sense of loyalty again would not permit him to accept. It was not until *El liberal* folded in 1923 that he felt morally free to go to *El Sol.* This rather naive approach to financial matters characterized Gómez de la Serna all his life.[22] When Ramón's father died in 1922, he left the young writer a modest inheritance, which, together with the generous income he received from *El Sol,* placed him in a better financial situation than he had ever known. Ramón moved to the tower apartment that was to become famed as his *torreón.*

Soon, however, he decided that the time had come to build the home of his dreams in Estoril. The young writer invested everything he had in the building of this retreat: the modest inheritance from his father, a substantial sum won in the National Lottery, and some money received for French translations of his works. He relied upon his fixed income from *El Sol* to meet the mortgage payments on this home (which he named "El Ventanal") and continued to live in the *torreón* while his new home was under construction.

The following year, when the dictatorship of Primo de Rivera was proclaimed, Ramón simultaneously removed himself from the political intrigues of the capital and supplemented his income by making a lecture tour of the provinces. In the course of this tour, the "Circo americano" gave a special performance to honor him for his book on the circus, and Ramón, in a flamboyant and typically vanguardist gesture, reciprocated with a lecture delivered from a trapeze in the circus arena.

VI *Ramón's Growing Influence and Prestige*

More important for the young writer's future, however, than either the lecture tour or the circus lecture which took place in 1923, was the fact that Ortega y Gasset founded the *Revista de Occidente* and solicited Ramón's contributions to the magazine. This new association with the *Revista* not only brought him generous fees; it also furthered his friendship with the German-educated, Krausist-influenced Ortega. The Krausist philosophy had incited a group of Spanish intellectuals, including Ortega, to seek new forms of life for themselves and their country through a regenerative educational program. In addition to Spanish men of letters, the program envisioned the introduction into Spain of the best in European thought; Ortega was the first in his country to print the works of Kafka, Huxley, Lawrence, Spengler, Jung, and Keyserling.[23]

Ramón often met Ortega in the offices of the magazine and in the *tertulia* which the *Revista de Occidente* held in a rented room on the Gran Vía. A warm cordiality developed between the two, despite the fact that in many ways they were exact opposites. Ortega was the methodical thinker and great literary stylist; Ramón was the impulsive, irrational emotionalist who, in his eagerness to express himself, considered style a relatively unimportant element of composition. Sainz de Robles, one of the few critics who has taken cognizance of the association between Ramón and Ortega, believes that their mutual appreciation derived from the deep sincerity they saw in one another,[24] and Julián Marías (who maintains that in Ramón's generation, only three men reached the status of genius: Ortega in philosophy, Picasso in art, and Ramón in literature) affirms that Ramón, who was not an intellectual, was influenced by Ortega.[25]

Even before their association at the *Revista de Occidente,* Gómez de la Serna manifested his admiration for Ortega by dedicating *El secreto del acueducto (The Secret of the Aqueduct)* to him because he felt that the truths Ortega told in such a limpid style were as old as the aqueduct of Segovia, yet were pertinent to the present and future. In this, as in most of Ramón's novels, people recede to the background, and things become the focus of attention. A slim thread of a story serves Ramón as a pretext for invoking the historical and legendary atmosphere of Segovia, and the aqueduct fascinates him to the extent that, at several points in the book, he becomes wholly absorbed in it, paying it strings of compliments or *piropos.*

Through this personification of the inanimate, the exaltation of things and the inversion of values, Ramón accomplished in fact what Ortega had proposed in theory when, in 1925, he advocated the "dehumanization" of art, an upsetting of traditional value patterns to produce "an art in which small events of life appear in the foreground with monumental dimensions. . . . a study of the microstructure of life."[26]

The "microstructure" described by Ortega fascinated Ramón to such an extent that throughout his life he produced occasional books dealing wholly with minutiae: *Muestrarios (Samplings)*. 1918, *Variaciones (Variations),* 1920, *Virguerías (Virginal Glimpses),* 1920, *Disparates (Absurdities),* 1921, *Ramonismo (Ramonism),* 1923, *Caprichos (Caprices),* 1924, *Gollerías (Tidbits),* 1926, and *Trampantojos (Tricks of Whimsy),* 1947. Perhaps the best of these books was *Ramonism,* written, as Ramón said, to "oppose my ISM to all the other ISMS."[27] Like the other books in this category, *Ramonism* is a collection of light, varied, and extremely fanciful thoughts on random and inconsequential subjects such as: parrots, kiosks, awnings, empty lots, polka dot blouses, and models of absurd letters for all occasions. It even includes an essay on "being an etcetera":

> There are moments when one is an etcetera. We have all, at some time, been etceteras. Who has not experienced this threat of anonymity and hodgepodge?
> Present were Mr. X, Mr. Y, etcetera.
> "Had one more name been listed, ours would have appeared," we delude ourselves.
> "Surely someone will perceive that I am included in this etcetera," one tells oneself, to console oneself, not to see oneself so lost, so unjustly treated, so boxed in by these incongruent letters. . . .
> But no, no one notices. It is a vain illusion to think that we can poke our noses out from behind an etcetera. . . .[28]

Sometimes when Ramón personified inanimate objects, he whimsically endowed them with erotic tendencies. The result, as in his tale of the statues perverted by the application of fig leaves, is a highly humorous parody of life:

> The official with dark glasses ordered that fig leaves be placed on all statues, large fig leaves. . . . A million *duros* was voted for the work.
> The imposition of fig leaves on all the statues was celebrated with great solemnity. Numerous ladies from various organizations attended, and members of the major confraternities. The imposter — or is it imposer? — of the fig leaves used a white lacquer to affix them. . . . The statues looked at the fig leaves, and, feeling a slight tickle, like that which a comedian feels on his lip, beneath a false moustache, scratched themselves inconspicuously. This act of scratching themselves compromised their innocence. They had never moved, they had never looked at themselves, they had never touched themselves, but the attention which the fig leaves awakened in them, made Art lose its serenity. . . . they lost their ingenuousness . . . they became perverted.[29]

It is curious that, despite its frequent appearance in his works, this mixture of fantasy and eroticism in Ramón has not been more commented upon by critics. Its most extreme expression is attained in *El hombre perdido (The Lost Man)* when the unnamed protagonist becomes enamored of the plumbing fixtures in his bathroom. In dealing with the sensual and the sexual, as with everything else, Ramón transformed them by his wondrous imaginative powers.

La quinta de Palmyra (Palmyra's Country Villa), Cinelandia (Movieland), and *El novelista (The Novelist)* also appeared in 1923, making it a year of unprecedented productivity and prosperity for Ramón. The first was a sensuous tale told against a Portuguese background; the second was a story of movieland, and the third was, in some respects, an autobiographical novel. In it, Ramón dealt more with his protagonist's literary creation than with his biography, presenting over twenty plots in partially developed or embryonic stages which his novelist had completed, was working on, or had projected. This book is, above all, interesting for the insight it provides into the crowded fertile mind of a writer.

VII A New Life

Ramón's well-being came to an abrupt end when *El Sol* found that it could no longer afford to pay fixed salaries to its contributors. Without the regular salary he had depended upon, Ramón was unable to meet mortgage payments on El Ventanal and was forced to sell it, along with all the rest of his possessions, at an enormous loss. After that, he literally fled to Naples where he planned to settle permanently.

Perhaps Naples made the young man homesick for Spain or perhaps his recent bitter experiences turned his mind to the constant battles and stark realities of life, for he now wrote *El torero Caracho (Caracho the Toreador)*, a novel about that very Spanish phenomenon — the bullfight. It is an unusual work, showing Ramón's deep feeling for both life and death. Before he could publish it, however, Ramón, unable to pay his rent and other debts, as inconspicuously as possible, left Naples for Madrid.

During the next few years, his activities were sporadic. His finances improved in 1928 with the offer of a paying column in *La Nación*, and with the translation of some of his works into French — *La vueve blanche et noire, Seins, Le cirque, Le docteur invraisemblable,* and *Gustavo l'incongru*. The last two works, called in Spanish *El doctor inverosímil* and *El incongruente* (in English, respectively, *The Unlikely Doctor* and *The Incongruent One)*, are worthy of note. Although Ramón called the first a "short novel," it is more like a collection of short stories written about Doctor Vivar — whose name is itself a play on the verb *vivir* (to live). Ramón's "unlikely doctor" examines his patients by probing into their pasts and treats them more or less successfully by helping them discard old memories and souvenirs. Since Ramón wrote this book in 1914, long before the general public was familiar with psychoanalysis, psychosomatic medicine or allergies, his insight in these matters is astonishing.

With Gustavo, "the incongruent one," Ramón entered boldly the realm of the surreal which he had previously penetrated occasionally with his *greguerías*. His protagonist has no personal ties, no responsibilities; his life has no order, logic, or goal; it merely, incongruously, "happens" to him. His dreams are even more fantastic than his life, for in them he experiences sensations even more weird: "So incongruous were his dreams that he sometimes started out old in them, regressed to childhood, and eventually returned to the maternal womb to die before coming forth."[30] His incongruous existence ends, however, when he establishes a tie with reality through marriage. Cardona points out that this book appeared in 1922, fully six years before The Frenchman Breton's *Nadja*.[31] Thus, in the realm of the surreal, as in the realm of things, Ramón may be considered a precursor.

The translation of these works occasioned another visit to Paris where Ramón found that his popularity was high. When he established a literary *tertulia* at the Café des Vickings et de la Rotonde, writers and critics like Cami, Cassau, Larbaud, and Max Jacob as well as foreigners flocked to it as if it were Pombo. The winter circus gave a special performance to honor the writer of *Le cirque,* and Ramón reciprocated as he had in Spain, with a discourse for the occasion. This time he did what he had yearned to do before, and gave his speech seated on the back of a circus elephant! Although the flamboyant gesture was typical of Ramón at this period, there was a sincerity in it too. It was his way of making himself one with the circus he so keenly enjoyed.

VIII *His Wanderings*

From Paris, Ramón returned to Madrid, and within the next few years produced *La mujer de ámbar (The Amber Woman),* 1927, *El caballero del hongo gris (The Gentleman in the Grey Top Hat),* 1928, and *Goya,* also of 1928, along with scores of lesser works. In 1928, he collected some biographical sketches which had previously appeared as prologues, and published them in a volume called *Efigies (Effigies).* With the publication of this work, Gómez de la Serna took a major step in the direction of biographical writing. Biographical studies, both long and short, were thereafter to comprise a major portion of his work.

In 1929, Ramón tried his hand at theater with *Los medios seres (The Half-Beings)*, a play in which the characters appeared with one normal side and one black side, representing their black, negative, or deficient qualities. The idea for this play had come to him while contemplating the portrait of "La muerta viva" ("The living dead woman") in his study, a portrait of a woman showing one-half of her face and form beautiful and alive, the other half decayed and skeletal. Although the play aroused a stir in Madrid, it was not a success. Wounded by unfavorable reviews and piqued by the "half and half" practical jokes made at his expense, Ramón left Madrid for Paris, resolved to present no more theatrical works.

At first it seemed that his former great popularity was to be repeated. He had written a prologue for a posthumous book of Apollinaire's which made all Paris smile benignly upon him.[32] He was the guest of honor at countless banquets, dinners, and *soirées*. Now, however, his heightened sensitivity perceived a snobbishness in these invitations which repelled him. He felt humiliated by the very hosts who wined and dined him, and came to believe that they treated him more as a servant brought in to entertain, than as a guest. He began to refuse many invitations and to attend only those that he truly enjoyed, such as literary *tertulias* and meetings of the French Academy of Humor.

When lack of funds became a pressing problem, Ramón went to Berlin where he had heard that lectures would be more remunerative. But Berlin was cold and audiences small. When his funds were completely exhausted, an invitation to speak in Barcelona provided him train fare back to Spain. From Barcelona, he made his way to Madrid. There, although political instability had heightened with the fall of Primo de Rivera's dictatorship, Ramón, like many Spaniards in those days, hoped for the dawning of a new era.

In October, 1930, Ramón ventured into another medium of expression and inaugurated a series of late night radio chats broadcast directly from his study. These chats, well received by the public, were largely spontaneous and improvised, somewhat comparable to the unrehearsed late night programs so popular on television today.

In 1931, a few months before the Republic was proclaimed, when Ortega and a group of other writers left *El Sol* because of differences with the paper's promonarchical policy, Ramón left with them, more for friendship's sake than for political reasons.[33] The change worsened his already bad financial situation. He reached the point where he could not afford heat, ate irregularly, and the Saturday meetings at Pombo came to embarrassing conclusions when he and his friends faced the painful moment of paying the tab.[34]

Although the advent of the Republic seemed to promise a great future for the development of intellectual life and liberty in Spain, it in no way alleviated Ramón's pressing financial problems. When an offer came to him from the Amigos de Arte de Buenos Aires to give a series of lectures there, Ramón was not only free, but eager to accept.

Not long after his arrival in Argentina, Ramón met Luisa Sofovich, a lovely young writer of Russian-Jewish origin who was separated from her husband and had an infant son. Shortly after her divorce was settled, Ramón took her back to Madrid with him as his wife.

He gave a series of conferences in the provinces so that he could show Luisa his country, but when this tour ended, the financial troubles that were to plague him for the rest of his life set in once more. In 1933, accompanied by Luisa, he returned to Buenos Aires to deliver another series of lectures. His speeches, humorously novel before, became even more so now, as he utilized both costuming effects and "gimmicks" to entertain his audiences.

When they returned to Spain after this trip Luisa contracted an illness that brought her close to death. Writing feverishly to meet the expenses incurred by her illness, he produced his poetically beautiful biography, *El Greco,* and completed *Los muertos y las muertas (Dead Men and Dead Women),* a work he had begun thirteen years earlier. In this work Ramón assembled comments on death by famous men of all cultures and eras, including, for example, Seneca, Marcus Aurelius, Pyrrhus, Omar Khayyám, Pascal, and Schopenhauer. He set down choice tombstone epitaphs and added his own reflections on death. He appended a second part to the book, a collection of macabre stores which he called *Otras fantasmagorías (Other Phantasmagories),* and the two were published as one volume in 1935.

This work reveals the affectionate familiarity with death characteristic of Ramón. In novels like *Caracho the Toreador, La Nardo (The Spikenard),* 1930 — in which lovers try to preserve their love by an act of double suicide — and *El hombre perdido (The Lost Man),* 1947 — where the protagonist lives and dies in anonymity — and also in his biographies of Nerval (in *Efigies,* 1929), *Quevedo* (1935), and *Poe* (1963); in his *Greguerías,* and in his very deliberately named *Automoribundia (Autodeathography),* Ramón returns constantly to the theme of death as if fascinated by it. He saw a positive value in death's quickening "the vital restlessness" of life.[35] In a typically "ramonesque" gesture, he dedicated this book on death to the doctor (Carlos Maortua) who had saved Luisa's life.

The income from these works helped Ramón to pay his most pressing debts, and then, once his preoccupation with his own distressing problems had lessened, he became aware of the restlessness in Madrid. Tempers were short, even at Pombo, where political discussions had long been outlawed, and one night, on returning from the *tertulia* he had so long nurtured, Ramón observed sadly to Luisa that he would have to discontinue his *tertulia*.[36] About three months later, the revolution broke out. Dreading violence, Ramón cast about for a pretext to leave Spain. As co-founder of the P.E.N. Club in Madrid, he took advantage of the congress which that club was holding in Buenos Aires to obtain a passport, sent ahead the books he had written, and left Spain. He arrived in Buenos Aires with Luisa, a few personal possessions, unflagging faith in himself, and an enormous capacity for work.

IX *The Expatriate*

Oliverio Girondo, an old friend, prudently discouraged the new immigrant from delivering a series of radio talks about the revolution, and lent him instead the sum the talks would have brought. With this money plus a small income from a column in *La Nación* and fees from occasional articles elsewhere, Gómez de la Serna managed to support himself and Luisa from one day to the next. Latin-American publications paid less than those in Spain, and Ramón soon found that in order to survive he had to work even longer hours than in Madrid. He had not expected his beginnings in America to be so difficult.

At the beginning of their stay in Buenos Aires, he and Luisa frequented social gatherings at the Embassy and elsewhere, but later, unable to keep up the appearances these social events demanded, they declined such invitations. Ramón also became increasingly disinclined to give lectures, feeling that the stipend he received did not compensate for his time and for the anxiety such talks caused him. He felt, moreover, that the public was not as receptive to him as it once had been.

The less he ventured into society, the more it abandoned him. As Ramón's isolation from others increased, his devotion to Luisa, which had always been somewhat excessive, grew proportionately. His possessiveness exceeded jealousy. Whenever they attended any gatherings, he would stay as close as possible to her side, and became querulous if she left the room. He all but clung to her skirt much as a pampered child clings to his mother and refuses to let her out of sight.[37] In love, as in literature, there was an abiding childlikeness about Ramón.

Continued economic pressures forced the harried writer to grind out even more articles, interfered with his writing books and reduced him even to writing blurbs. Thus, despite his prodigious capacity for work, Gómez de la Serna published fewer books than usual in those early years in Buenos Aires. These included ¡Rebeca! (which had been written previously, but wasn't published until 1936), the first collection of *Retratos contemporáneos (Contemporary Portraits),* 1941, *Mi tía Carolina Coronado (My Aunt Carolina Coronado),* 1942, *Don Diego Velázquez,* 1943, *Maruja Mallo,* 1943, and *Doña Juana la loca (Doña Juana the Mad),* 1944.

¡*Rebeca!* deserves the exclamation points Ramón gave it. The work he so correctly called his first completely nebulous novel had even less continuity and cohesion than *The Incongruent One.* The theme, reminiscent of Villiers' search for the ideal woman, is the protagonist's search for "Rebeca." In the course of the novel, "Rebeca" assumes various erotic forms, but never becomes specific and it is never clear whether "Rebeca" is *a* woman, *the* woman, or an ideal. In the end, the protagonist, Luis, ceases hunting the unobtainable and settles for the real woman he can obtain. The story could easily be an oblique retelling of Ramón's personal search for the ideal woman and his marriage to Luisa.

In *Doña Juana the Mad,* Ramón applied his unreal touch to history in a series of six "superhistorical novels" constructed largely on "subconscious facts," capriciously changing the traditional stories of his subjects, and working havoc with the hitherto untarnished reputations of legendary heroes like the Siete Infantes de Lara (Seven Princes of Lara) and the Caballero de Olmedo (Gentleman from Olmedo).

Between 1944 and 1948, Ramón completed some of the original works he had been laboring over for years: *Nuevos retratos contemporáneos (New Contemporary Portraits), José Gutiérrez Solana, Don Ramón María del Valle-Inclán, Lope viviente (The Living Lope),* and his mammoth *Automoribundia (Autodeathography),* all clearly indicating his increased preoccupation with biography. In his growing isolation in America, Ramón, as Antonio Valencia has noted, seems to have withdrawn even more into himself and his memories:

> "[In America] he now turns inward and to memory . . . . The biographic sketch became much more important in his work in America than it had been before. With it, Ramón became much more profound and through biographies of others revealed his work and his literary self to us, offering us, thus, a final perspective of his worth and being."[38]

X The Final Years

In 1949, Pedro Rocamora, then president of the Ateneo of Madrid, invited Ramón to visit that city. Filled with optimistic illusions, the sixty-year-old writer accepted. A favorable press heralded his impending visit and when he debarked, he was greeted by friends, relatives, political officials, and press representatives. Madrid welcomed him with banquets, plays, interviews, and official visits; city officials solemnly placed a plaque on the façade of the house where he had been born. Overcome with emotion, Ramón announced his intention to return permanently to Spain within a few years. From Madrid he went to Barcelona where he gave more conferences and interviews. But a strange thing happened. When Ramón returned to Bilbao to board ship for Buenos Aires, none of his literary friends came to see him off.

Their fervor had cooled and they left him in pointed isolation largely because of some completely unsolicited statements he had made in the course of his visit, in favor of the Franco regime. Actually, without realizing it, five years earlier when he had accepted the offer of a regular column in *Arriba,* a pro-Franco newspaper, Ramón had appeared to many to commit himself to the Franco regime. His remarks now seemed to confirm that position. It was a pity that anyone should have attached importance to anything Gómez de la Serna said about politics, for he was, in the fullest sense of the word, apolitical. He lived in a world of his own, a world of fantasy, completely removed from politics. On the few occasions when he did make naîve political comments, his remarks unfortunately had disastrous repercussions.

Despite the fact that the writer's trip to Spain coincided with the publication of *Las tres gracias (The Three Graces)* and *Cartas a las golondrinas (Letters to the Swallows),* it depleted his resources. On his return to Buenos Aires, he once more put aside manuscripts on which he had been working (biographies of Quevedo, Poe and

Unamuno) in order to grind out the faster-paying articles without which he could not have survived. *Quevedo* and *Edgar Poe, el genio de América (Edgar Poe, the Genius of America)* he managed to publish before the end of that year, but his work on Unamuno was never finished.

The approach of 1954, the fiftieth anniversary of his literary career, brought speculation concerning the possibility of Ramón's return to Madrid from Argentina. Although the subject was repeatedly broached to him, he was still wounded by the incident of 1949 and would not consider it.

Despite his refusal to return to Spain, Ramón nevertheless received countless honors in the form of special issues, dedications, and tributes in magazines and newspapers there as well as in the Latin-American press. A few years later, in 1956, *Nostalgias de Madrid (Nostalgias of Madrid)* appeared, bearing witness to his feeling for his native city. In it, Ramón returned to Madrid at least in memory, capturing many of the simple things that were part and parcel of it: the nursemaids in the park, the plazas, fountains, monuments, and streets of the city. In a moving portion of the book called "Letanía de Madrid," ("Madrid Litany"), Ramón enumerated the simple things that for him comprised the city's essence:

Madrid is a file of tourists entering the Museum with huge suitcases full of admiration in hand.

It is the atmosphere of a spring fair [. . .]

It is knowing that the breeze is blowing from the Plaza de Oriente . . .

It is a collection of ingenious people working the miracle of living on a piece of gold willed to them by their grandmothers . . .

Madrid is passing through the Puerta del Sol as if it were there that one could find the holy water font for each day's blessing . . .[39]

A group of Spanish writers was stimulated by the occasion of Ramón's literary anniversary to initiate a movement for his candidacy for the Nobel Prize. Forestalling disillusionment, Ramón wrote to his cousin Gasper, discouraging the project. "About the Nobel," he said, "if I have any good friend who persists in that illusion, thank him for it, and dissuade him."[40]

In Ramón's jubilee year, *Lope viviente (The Living Lope)* was finally published; Aguilar contracted for an anniversary edition of *Greguerías completas (Complete Greguerías)*; AHR of Barcelona prepared to publish his *Obras completas (Complete Works)*, and a number of Latin-American publishing companies collaborated in bringing forth an *Antologia (Anthology)* of his works. Yet, from the standpoint of his personal life, Ramón considered the most significant happening of that jubilee year to be his return to the practice of his religion. In *Automoribundia (Autodeathography)*, he had revealed a sincere return to the religious beliefs of his childhood. Now he went further and returned to religious practice.[41]

The aging writer was not to enjoy this state of well-being very long, for Perón's downfall in Argentina in 1955 had totally unforeseen repercussions in his life. During Ramón's 1949 visit to Spain, in addition to his statements about the Franco regime, Ramón had also praised Perón for the pro-Franco sympathies he had exhibited in the '40's. With Perón's downfall, those words were remembered, and a number of papers either severed associations with him or neglected to pay him for his articles. Again the problem of whether or not to return to Spain faced him, and once again Ramón elected to remain in Buenos Aires. His financial need now was greater than before, and he was beginning to feel the pressure of his long hours of writing. "In July I shall be seventy," he wrote to Gaspar, "and I am under as much pressure as if I were twenty-nine." "My *greguerías* come a little harder now."[42]

Once more Ramón received a formal invitation to Madrid — this time to receive the Grand Cross of Alfonso X, and once again he refused. By now he was forced to admit that the journey was beyond his physical powers. In a letter to Tomás Borrás, he wrote, "I am a little tired now. My eight or ten monthly articles and my four or five groups of forty *greguerías* each month now weigh heavily upon me."[43]

He now began to dream great dreams as a child would, of a magnificent award, like the Premio March (March Award), carrying with it the half million pesetas that would allow him to live happily ever after. "When one least expects it, even though it may be late, a surprisingly theatrical breakthrough sometimes happens," he wrote, full of illusion, to Gaspar.[44] In 1960, although he received a minor prize, the Juan Palomo Award, the coveted grand prize eluded him. He was by now suffering from arteriosclerosis and diabetes. Father Félix García and Tomás Borrás, both his lifelong friends, were appalled by the thought of the financial burden illness would place upon him and they worked ceaselessly at pricking both consciences and pocketbooks in Madrid and Buenos Aires on his behalf.

They maneuvered unsuccessfully to capture the March Award for him in 1959, in 1960, and again in 1961. Then, a "special" March Award of three hundred thousand pesetas was awarded him in a "special convocation" on January 31, 1962. Two other awards followed from Galicia and Catalonia, and finally the Argentine Parliament awarded him a monthly pension of five thousand pesos for the rest of his life in recognition of his literary achievements.

The persistent labors of Tomás Borrás and Padre Félix finally bore fruit on April 9, 1962, when the March Award jury unanimously chose Ramón Gómez de la Serna as the receipient of that year's official award. Although Ramón was hospitalized in Buenos Aires when this news reached him, his moral and physical condition improved immediately, and he began formulating fantastic projects for a highly improbable future. His optimism did not deceive Luisa. She realized that he was no longer physically able to bear the strain of meeting publication deadlines and she took it upon herself to meet his publishing obligations by searching through old diaries and notebooks for unpublished *greguerías* which she sent to newspapers awaiting deliveries of Ramón's manuscripts.

During the night of January 12, 1963, Ramón died quietly. His body was viewed by an endless procession of people and on January 14, he was buried in the Recoleta cemetery of Buenos Aires. A flood of necrologic and eulogistic articles appeared in the Spanish and Latin-American press, and the City Council of Madrid voted to have his body transported there and accorded posthumous honors.

His remains were flown to Madrid. There, after a final tribute from the people of his native city, Ramón was interred in the Panteón de Hombres Ilustres where Larra, Espronceda, Bretón de los Herreros, and other Spanish writers are buried. With this final act, Gómez de la Serna finally received the recognition he had so consistently sought during his life.

When he felt death drawing near, Ramón had written to Padre Félix García, "I feel . . . that my death is near . . . If I did not have the counterbalance of God, I should weaken. How necessary God is for life! But he is even more necessary for death!"[45]

When he died, Ramón Gómez de la Serna left unfinished a book that he was writing on the subject of his return to God. If it is ever published, then, at last, his *Autodeathology* will have its final chapter and the story of his "living unto death" will be complete.

CHAPTER 2

Fiction: Articles, Essays, Drama, Pantomimes

I Articles and Essays

BECAUSE of Gómez de la Serna's unique literary style, the thousands of articles and essays he wrote throughout his long lifetime for many newspapers and magazines may rightly be considered a prime example of his creative writing. To attempt a systematic and complete bibliographical compilation of these works would be an almost impossible task, for Ramón, in his sometimes dire need of money, not only wrote countless articles, he also reworked, combined, altered, or otherwise edited articles previously published and sent them off to other publishers for further publication. For years he wrote essay columns for *La Tribuna, El liberal, El Sol,* and *Arriba* as well as frequent articles for other newspapers and magazines in Spain, Argentina, Chile, Colombia, Cuba, and other Latin-American countries — wherever, in brief, they found a publisher.

Some of his biographical sketches first appeared as essays in *Revista de Occidente,* or as prologues to translations or selected works of the writers studied and later reappeared as sections or chapters of longer biographical works. This occurred, for instance, with his studies on Goya, Quevedo, Lope de Vega, Valle-Inclán, Azorín, Ortega, Dalí, and Picasso among others.

Some of his published essays were later collected into a volume entitled *Lo cursi y otros ensayos* (Affectations and Other Essays). Still others reappeared in his works on Madrid or Buenos Aires. And hundreds of others remain simply as articles in far-flung publications. These articles not only include essays on literature, pictorial art, and personalities from both those areas; they also embrace everything and anything that caught Ramón's whimsical fancy, or intrigued his childlike interest and curiosity. They include such varied subjects as algae, art, ballet, bullfighting, butterflies, crystal balls, chimneys, the

Fiction: Articles, Essays, Drama, Pantomimes [37]

cinema, doors and doorways, factories, fish, flowers, handkerchiefs, humor, door knockers, literary banquets, manic depressives, metaphors, monuments, mosquitoes, mural painting, names of women, night, the pampa, peons, phrenology, psychiatry, psychoanalysis, realism, romanticism, shops and shop windows, starfish, syphons, streets and street names, time and clocks, trees and words, and they have appeared in magazines and newspapers such as *Revista de Occidente, Temas, Cruz y Raya, El Universal, Revista, Clavileño, Saber vivir, Buen Humor, El Hogar, El Heraldo* and *Arriba,* among others.

II *Drama*

Among Gómez de la Serna's earliest works were a number of dramas, written in a period of fervent obsession with the dramatic genre, when he was between the ages of nineteen and twenty-one. Most were published in his own magazine, *Prometeo,* some in *Revista de Occidente,* or other magazines, and a few appeared in limited cheap editions. Although he maintained that he never intended their presentation,[1] Ramón nevertheless admitted sending a collection of them to a popular Spanish actor for criticism. The actor returned them with the comment that they were "good but unstageable."[2]

Because Ramón did not have the patience for a gradual building up of plot, he preferred to write short plays, and even pantomimes, concentrating on the dramatic moment of truth, revelation, or decision that intrigued him. Consequently, most of his dramatizations are imaginative one-act pieces. His characters are, typically, strange types like "the man with no eyebrows," "the girl with the glass eye," "the woman with hands of gold,"[3] the "half-beings" or even the unfulfilled or nostalgic dead. His embryonic plots embrace a wide variety of subjects.

Beatriz, for example, portrays an ardent follower of John the Baptist who deliberately seeks leprous contamination in a prison cell to join the adored Master in death. *Utopía (Utopia)* presents a sculptor who, prevented from sculpting his dreamed-of masterpiece, "Utopia," because of the frustrating necessity of sculpting endless "pretty" statues to earn a living, finally shoots himself. *El palacio deshabitado (The Uninhabited Palace)* takes place in a tomb beneath a palace. All but two of the characters are dead, and the dialogue consists either of expressions of regret at unfulfilled desires, or nostalgic remembrances of desires fulfilled. *Desolación (Desolation)* tells the story of fourteen-year-old Solita's experience as her governess's confidante concerning her doomed love for a dying man. *Cuento de callejo (Alley Tale)*, a children's play, concerns a child's first disillusionment. *El laberinto (The Labyrinth)* is a symbolic drama in which a desolate group of young women wandering in the labyrinthine paths of a Madrid park, exchange confidences on their lost virginity and subsequent abandonment by their seducers. *El lunático (The Madman)* is about a young man who falls in love with a woman's velvet masquerade mask. When a young lady, a family friend, dons the mask, hoping to divert his attention from it to herself, he is unexpectedly overcome with desire for the now animated mask, and accosts her. She resists his passionate advances and he unwittingly strangles her. The mask, inert again, loses its hypnotic appeal for him. *Los sonámbulos (The Sleepwalkers)* is somewhat reminiscent of the Dance of Death as its cast of varied characters, an old woman, a young girl, a gambler, a virgin, a money-lender, a just man, all dialogue with Christ in Heaven. It differs in that all awaken, embarrassed, to find that they have been dreaming in the presence of others, In *Tránsito (Transition)*, Susana, an aging actress, after anxiously studying herself in a mirror, tacitly admits that she is aging, by telling her young lover that her next part will be a character role. After she has silenced his protests, and he leaves, she dons a white wig, contemplates herself in the mirror, and then pensively seats herself in an armchair as the curtain closes. *Los unánimes (The Unanimous Ones)* is a confusing scene, in which a heterogeneous group of "marginal" characters, gathered in an untraveled city street, discuss both light and serious matters. Informed that disaster has struck the city, they line up to pass through a great doorway into . . . What? Perhaps the great beyond. The conclusion is not clear and the work is ambiguous.

A two-act drama, *Siempreviva (Ever Alive;* The *siempreviva* is also a flower, the "Forget-me-not") presents Andrés, a grief-stricken widower, vowing, in the first act, to keep the memory of his beautiful young wife ever alive. In Act Two, his best friend, Cruz, tells him that he was the dead woman's lover, and disputes with him his right to a widower's grief. While they are speaking, a third man arrives, also claiming to have loved her, and carrying "her favorite perfume" — a scent unfamiliar to the other two!

Two three-act plays, *La corona de hierro (Crown of Iron)* and *La Casa Nueva (The New House)* appeared in 1911. The first has all the accouterments of Modernism: morbidity, royalty, gardens, etc. In

Act One, the king's loneliness is established, and he plans to meet his mistress at a country palace. Act Two takes place in the country palace. Christian, the king's mistress, is unhappy in the dark and morbid palace. Later, piqued because someone has sent a bouquet of flowers to the king, she leaves. In Act Three, when the queen's new portrait is presented to him, the king realizes anew her beauty, perfections, strength, and ability to sustain him and the "Crown of Iron" (kingship) he bears upon his brow. His love for her is reborn, and the play ends with the reconciled couple contentedly playing a game of chess.

In *The New House,* Don Severo plans, in Act One, to build a large house with a tower, lake, many rooms, paintings, gardens, and so on. In Act Two, a dance is held in the new house, and delightful conversations take place between the young townswomen and young men from the city. In Act Three, Don Severo nostalgically remembers his old home, where his parents and grandparents died, and his family had its roots. He decides to return there, leaving the new house empty, its rooms and gardens sterile.

Teatro en soledad (Theater in Solitude), written the following year, shows Ramón's familiarity with the theater and its jargon, and his pre-Pirandellian attempts at experimentation. It begins in a deserted theater, where, following a play, the actors gather onstage and discuss their performance. When they leave, the characters of the play come forth from the darkened stage, criticizing the evening's poor performance. In Act Two, the characters stage their own play-within-the-play. After most of the actors have left, the play's lead actor and its femme fatale indulge in an amorous exchange which is interrupted by the hammering of stagehands. Act Three presents another set of actors discussing the problems of drama in general and expressing their desire for a new and better play in which to perform.

Two more three-act plays were written when Gómez de la Serna was more mature. *Los medios seres (The Half-Beings),* 1929, the only one of Ramón's dramas to reach the stage, presented characters whose forms were half normal and half black, representing the fact that most people are unwittingly incomplete or lacking in some qualities. It was evidently an attempt at more sophisticated theater, dealing with the beginning of extramarital affairs by both husband and wife on the occasion of their first wedding anniversary. The dialogue, full of "greguerístic" nonsequiturs, is difficult to read, and must have been even more difficult to stage. The play was not a success, and after it, tired of the half-and-half jokes even his friends couldn't resist perpetrating on him, Ramón vowed to publish no more dramas. He broke that vow, however, six years later.

In 1935, he published *Las escaleras (The Stairways)*. In this drama, as the characters arrive at an ambiguous address in answer to a newspaper advertisement, they must decide which of two stairways leading to adjacent houses they should ascend. Once again, those choosing the stairway on the left find themselves in the "house of happiness"; those on the right, in the "house of sadness." Luisa violates all rules when she commits the unheard-of act of leaving the house of happiness to join her lover who had chosen the other stairway. As they embrace, joyful at being reunited, the polarities of joy and sadness change; the sad house becomes happy and the happy one sad.

III *Pantomimes*

In addition to his plays, Gómez de la Serna also wrote a series of little-known pantomimes, most of which were published in *Prometeo*. *La bailarina (The Dancer)*, is a pantomime in two parts. In the first part, Hamlet watches Ophelia perform; and in the second, she emerges from the theater in street clothes and, although attracted to Hamlet, is subsequently seduced by the impresario. *Las rosas rojas (Red Roses)* presents a nun undressing alone in her room, admiring her thick black hair in the mirror and then burying her head in a bouquet of red roses until they lose their petals. In *El nuevo amor (New Love)*, a lonely-seeming mestizo type comes onstage. A woman enters and dances around him, trying unsuccessfully to arouse his attention. Finally, she slashes her wrist, and he watches her slow immolation as, bleeding to death, she continues dancing before him. *Fiesta de Dolores (Sorrowful Fiesta)* presents a *bailarina* dressed in black who catches a bouquet of red carnations, holds them to her breast and then throws them violently away. She looks at her hands as if they were bloody, wrings them in her black head scarf, and then continues her dance. *Los dos espejos (Two Mirrors)* shows a lonely woman contemplating herself in a mirror. When a man draws near and kisses her, the mirror breaks. He leaves. Alone again, she takes out another mirror, and continues her self-contemplation. *Las danzas de la pasión, (Dances of Passion)*, a series of dance-pantomimes, includes: "La danza de los Apaches" ("Apache Dance"), a stylized love and mating dance; "La danza oriental" ("Oriental Dance"), a simple, poetically-written dance description of an oriental woman dancing alone, and "Los otros bailes" ("Other

Dances"), descriptions of other kinds of dances, some of highly stylized technical execution, fit for concerts, some apt for circuses, and so on.

In 1954, Ramón included several of his dramas when selecting works for inclusion in his *Obras completas (Complete Works)*, lamenting that they had never been staged, and complaining that many of his ideas had been taken by later dramatists.[4] Perhaps it is just as well that they were not performed. Their highly novelistic and poetic tone, replete with images and *greguerías*, provide interesting and delightful reading, but, unless presented simply as dramatic readings, they would be disastrously slow-paced for the stage, and their long poetic passages of description would be entirely lost.

CHAPTER 3

Fiction: Novels

IT is almost impossible to ascertain precisely the number of novels, novelettes, and short stories Ramón Gómez de la Serna has written. No two bibliographical lists agree completely, and occasional titles appear (or are mentioned by Ramón himself in texts elsewhere) that are untraceable. Moreover, critics often disagree as to the classification of his works, so that a title ascribed by one to the "novel" category, is listed by another as a "short novel," a "novelette," or even a "short story," so that the number of works cited in each group by different critics varies widely. Using length alone as a criterion, his "full-size" novels may be counted at eighteen. They may be divided basically into three categories: (1) those about places, ambients, or specific cities; (2) those that are deliberately nebulous, incongruous, unreal, or surreal; (3) those dealing primarily with disconnected events loosely strung together by a thin connecting thread.

In Ramón's fiction writing two things stand out: (1) all his works contain autobiographical elements; and, (2) all his works are surprisingly varied and different while remaining, somehow, paradoxically, very much the same. The "sameness" apparent in all of Ramón's works is unmistakable. They are alike in showing an imaginative, humorous, unreal world in which social, political, or moralizing elements never intrude. In these works (as indeed, in all that he wrote), Gómez de la Serna cultivated his own style: his capacity for observation, evocation, discovery, and intuition; his tendency to dehumanize persons and personify things, to equate the two or invert their importance by bringing things to the foreground. He delighted in things, sometimes interrupting his narrative for whole pages or even chapters to describe or merely list them or to include long series of *greguerías* and disjointed, nonsequential observations, comments, or "dialogue." Ramón's presence is constantly felt in everything he writes in the sense that all his works reflect his peculiar personality, vision, love of things, and concept of reality. Despite this, the reader never fully "captures" Ramón. He remains a free and elusive spirit, humorously mocking the seriousness with which the rest of the world regards "reality," and steadfastly refusing subservience to it in his essays, in his biographical works, and in his "superhistorical" works, and most assuredly, in his fiction.

Although the abundance of erotic or sensual elements in Ramón's stories is frequently commented upon or even censured by critics, except in a few instances (such as *Palmyra,* or *The Spikenard),* it is more *an* element than *the* element of his novels. Sometimes, as in *The Lost Man* or *The Incongruent One,* its treatment adds humor to the narration; sometimes, as in *Palmyra* or *¡Rebecca!* it adds an exotic or mysterious touch. Despite his abundance of sensuous scenes and incidents and references to sexual deviations considered taboo in the '20's, '30's and even '40's, Gómez de la Serna's erotic descriptions and references are never explicit, but are rather achieved through indirectness and innuendo. Neither is it the psychological state or problem they evoke which interests Ramón, for he never pretends to undertake a serious study of such things in his works. It is simply and superficially incongruity for its own sake — for the humor, charm, and novelty therein — that beguiles him.

Ramón's fictional heroes are generally like himself, free spirits, vagabond or bohemian types with no bonds, no past, no history, no future goals. Their function generally seems to be merely to wander through life, searching for, experiencing, and sometimes embodying new dimensions of reality and superreality. Sometimes this search for a different reality brings about their personification of the ambient. Sometimes, conversely, it leaves them rootless in an unreal environment. Often Ramón suggests rather than creates his characters, giving them minimal physical description and leaving them partly or even wholly nameless. His "lost man" has no name at all, and both Gustavo, his "incongruous" protagonist, and Lorenzo, his Spaniard wandering in Naples in the *Woman of Amber,* lack surnames. His characters are generally dehumanized, having no apparent motivation and demonstrating a humorously illogical behavior which reaches, at times, even to the surreal.

Often Gómez de la Serna's plots are no more than slim threads stringing together long series of whimsical, or even completely surreal experiences. Frequently they are subservient to atmosphere, stressing things or places rather than people, and disgressing into long pages or chapters of *greguerías* or prose poems. Like Azorín, Ramón in his novels often seems content not to go anywhere or to advance the story line at all, preferring simply to enjoy and deepen the moods or ambients he recreates. In *The Spikenard,* for example, he retards the story line by dedicating over a third of his pages to describing the *verbena*-like (carnival-like) atmosphere of Madrid in summertime, and in *Las tres gracias (The Three Graces)* he does the same, dedicating whole chapters to the jaunts of the three sisters of the title through the streets of Madrid, merely as a pretext for long, loving descriptions of that city.

For purposes of simplification and organization, Ramón's narrative works of fiction have here been divided arbitrarily (by length) into "Novels," "Novelettes," or "Short Stories," and "Novels" have been grouped by theme or treatment. Arrangement within each group is chronological. Gómez de la Serna's works are so numerous that only by some such arbitrary division can they be assimilated and examined.

I *Novels*

A. *Novels of Ambient*

In many of Gómez de la Serna's novels, plot and character are almost wholly subservient to locale and atmosphere. In these "novels of ambient" he tends both to idealize and to humanize his chosen locale, be it Portugal, Naples, Segovia, or Madrid. Curiously, since he seems to have written each of these novels when he was not in the locale described but elsewhere, his evocations are often nostalgic. He wrote *El torero Caracho (Caracho, the Toreador),* for example, (a novel about a bullfighter in Madrid) while he was in Naples; *Mujer de ámbar (The Amber Woman)* — about a woman who personified Naples — was written while he was in Madrid; *The Spikenard* (the story of a woman who incorporated the essence of Madrid) was written while he was in Paris, and *The Three Graces* and *Basement Flat* (both about Madrid) were written in Buenos Aires. This may explain the idealization and nostalgic evocation so noticeable in them.

In these novels, Ramón fuses the soul of his protagonist with the spirit of the locale, thereby dehumanizing the former and humanizing the latter. He gives more complete physical and spiritual descriptions of his settings than of his characters, imbuing them with personality (generally a feminine personality) as he speaks of their charm, sensuality, and even their "color." *The Spikenard,* for example, personifies the whiteness he associates with the spikenards of Madrid, and Lucía, his "woman of amber," evokes the amber-colored light of Naples. Frequently, Ramón makes a noteworthy landmark symbolic of a place's soul: for example, the Flea Market becomes a symbol of Madrid; Vesuvius, a symbol of Naples; the aqueduct, a symbol of Segovia. In each case, the symbolic object typifies the city and influences its characters. *La Nardo,* for example, sells herself cheaply in the marketplace of life much as she had once sold objects cheaply in the Rastro; Don Pablo, the protagonist of his novel about Segovia, is obsessed with the aqueduct; Lorenzo, the protagonist of his Neapolitan novel, with Vesuvius. Frequently, Ramón's female characters embody his locales, personifying their physical attributes, personality, even their subtle and intimate psychology. By possessing them, his male protagonists feel that they physically, erotically and somehow almost mystically, unite themselves with the place and ambient. In *La Nardo,* Ramón says plainly that the "best means of knowing the soul of Madrid was to set up house for the woman who incorporated the essence of its spirit."[1]

In his description of places, Gómez de la Serna indulges in personal familiarity with them by naming streets, plazas, monuments, parks, and so on, anxious, perhaps to convey his first-hand knowledge of places that were personally meaningful to him. Consequently, his descriptions become a curious blending of the impressionistic and the expressionistic as he attempts to present both the precise physical description his memory retains of these settings, and the subjective mental associations and impressions these places created in him. Like a skilled alchemist, he combines portions of objective and subjective memory with equal portions of nostalgia to produce delightfully gilded descriptions. Sometimes, when historical background influences his feelings for a locale or its personality, he presents it too. In each of these "novels of ambient," Ramón attempts to recreate personality and life of his settings, the aura and feeling that pervades them and the feelings they evoke. His locales are never "dead"; they are consciously infused with a vibrant, sometimes whimsical, life of their own.

1. La viuda blanca y negra (The Black and White Widow), *1918*

The Black and White Widow is the first work by Ramón that, for structure and length, rightly deserved to be considered a novel. In it, both Madrid and Paris ambients share honors as backgrounds for the story and actively affect Rodrigo's liaison with Cristina, an attractive young widow. Although her mourning greatly enhances her fair-skinned beauty and lends her an aura of mysterious dignity and poise, Rodrigo comes to suspect that she is not in actual fact a widow. Rumors lend substance to his doubts. When they visit Paris, his suspicions deepen, for, despite her pretense that this is her first visit to the French capital, numerous details betray her familiarity with it. Against the gay Parisian background, she becomes almost a "merry widow." Everything about her conduct confirms his suspicions. Shortly after their return to Madrid, when she receives a telegram advising her of the death of her husband, Rodrigo is disappointed to have the mystery ended. Cristina confesses that she had been merely separated from her husband, but had worn black both because of the liberty it gave her to go about Madrid alone, unmolested, and also because it was becoming to her. Disenchanted, Rodrigo casts about for a pretext for terminating their liaison and finds it in her refusal of his demand that she discontinue wearing black. Their affair ends in a scene of mutual recrimination and anger.

Rodrigo is the most ungallant of all of Ramón's heroes. Typically, in this early work as in his later ones, Ramón makes no moral judgments, but simply enjoys telling his story — in this case, a love story with a somewhat bizarre and morbid twist.

2. El secreto del acueducto (The Secret of the Aqueduct), *1922*

In Ramón's second novel of ambient, *The Secret of the Aqueduct,* (subtitled "The Novel of Segovia"), the locale comes to the fore. The plot, although well constructed, is a minor element of the narrative. Essentially, rather than a novel, this work is a chronicle of Segovia.

The story concerns Don Pablo, a middle-aged widower who marries his young housekeeper-niece, Rosario. Their wedding night is spent almost symbolically at a hotel in the shadow of the aqueduct, and all subsequent developments continue to be related to the city and the aqueduct. Marriage makes little change in their simple lives and relationship until money becomes a problem and they take in Pablo's priest-friend as a boarder. Then, Pablo, returning home unexpectedly one day, is surprised to hear voices in the bedroom and realizes that his wife and friend are having an affair. Thereafter, although he pretends to be unaware of the situation, he becomes obsessed with spying upon them, pretending to leave, reentering the house secretly and eavesdropping on the lovers from a hiding place in the next room. The tension upsets his already precarious mental equilibrium, and he begins to lose his hold on reality. Since the one thing that makes him important in Segovia is his knowledge of the town's history and his theories on the aqueduct's origin, he begins to display his knowledge incessantly and even accosts people to inform them about the city and the aqueduct. Adults and children alike begin to ridicule him and to consider him the town *loco*.

Don Pablo is the only well-developed character in the novel. It is the aqueduct, dominating both town and hero, that is the novel's true protagonist. Through his chronicles of the aqueduct Don Pablo believes he will achieve some measure of immortality. In this novel the aqueduct comes to symbolize eternity, or at least the antiquity so characteristic of Segovia.

3. La quinta de Palmyra (Palmyra's Country Villa), *1923*

Like much of Ramón's writing, this early novel is somewhat autobiographical in that it reflects the author's personal feeling for Portugal, a land he loved enough to make it the site of his "dream" house, and which he remembered with that blend of sadness and nostalgia the Portuguese call *saudade*. This is a brooding novel of moods, in which the sensuous and nostalgic protagonist personifies the atmosphere of Portugal.

Palmyra, a lonely, maturing woman, abandoned by a succession of lovers both because of her possessiveness and the isolation of her *quinta* (country estate), eventually realizes that only another woman will steadfastly remain with her. She thereupon invites a lesbian acquaintance to be her companion, finding in her the perfect combination of friend, lover, and lady-in-waiting that she has been seeking, someone willing to remain with her in the monotonous isolation of her estate. Gómez de la Serna, never indelicate, merely infers the relationship of the two women. Palmyra, a presence more than a person, is Ramón's personification of the aging, brooding, sensuous beauty of Portugal.

4. La mujer de ámbar (The Amber Woman), *1927*

In the prologue to this work, Ramón wrote that he did not wish to write a mere narrative, but that he desired to "evoke the unforgettable and eternal Naples."[2] He had sojourned three times in Naples before he wrote this work, traversing its streets in search of a woman who embodied its consciousness of eternity and the "amber" color of its sandy dust.

Lorenzo, the protagonist, like Ramón, is a Spaniard traveling in Naples, seeking the ideal Neapolitan woman. When he sees the lovely Lucía in a park, he feels that she embodies the soul of the city.

After idyllic strolls and meetings, he declares himself a serious suitor and is accepted as such by her relatives despite their long-standing hatred of Spaniards. As a gesture of good will, his prospective brother-in-law, Raffaelle, takes him on a tour of the city's bordellos, and even introduces him to Nazarena, his courtesan-mistress. Lorenzo becomes infatuated with her, and earns Raffaelle's hatred by possessing her. When Nazarena tells him that Lucía is not a virgin, but has mothered an illegitimate child, he investigates. Close-mouthed neighbors refuse to answer his questions, but, when he presses Lucía, she admits having had a twin sister, Lisa, who had been seduced by a Spaniard and had borne an illegitimate child. Her family had concealed the child's birth and repudiated Lisa. Intrigued by the story, Lorenzo seeks the twin, hoping she will serve as a substitute for the unyielding Lucía and save him from the necessity of marriage. Although he succeeds in this, he remains unsatisfied and realizes that only the lovely, amber-skinned Lucía can satisfy him for she alone embodies the spirit of Naples. On the day of the wedding, however, Lucía is apprehensive and confides to a friend that she is reluctant to marry a Spaniard and a foreigner. A few moments before the wedding, when she is briefly left alone in her room bedecked in her bridal gown, she commits suicide by throwing herself from the balcony. Lorenzo prudently disappears.

Ramón's protagonist, like himself at this period of his life, is free and unattached. He apparently has no purpose in Naples other than simply to be there. Unlike Ramón, he is a weak character, vacillating constantly between lofty ideals and sensuous desires. His persistent determination to "possess" the soul and spirit of Naples through the person of Lucía inexorably brings about the clash between two cultures which results in the final tragedy.

The carefully constructed plot seems largely contrived to provide a pretext for long conversations between the two lovers about the characteristic monuments and physical details of Naples, its women, its volcano, its historical past, and its atmosphere.

5. El torero Caracho (Caracho the Toreador), *1927*

While Gómez de la Serna was living in Naples, he wrote *Caracho,* a novel that came to be one of his most popular. It is the story of a bullfighter in Madrid. Perhaps an understandable nostalgia for his beloved native city influenced his choice of a theme so essentially Spanish. Critics stress the *españolismo* of this work, its very Spanish love of life and abiding consciousness of death.[3]

The protagonist, Caracho, has risen from poverty to riches as a toreador, in part through his own bravery and skill, and in part through the opportunities afforded him as the son-in-law of a famous torero. Insulted by his major rival, Cairel, he challenges him to a duel in which they wound one another, emerge with equal honor, and become firm friends. Invited to Portugal to give a demonstration fight on a national holiday, Caracho violates Portuguese custom by killing the bull. Enraged at the officials who had countenanced such brutality, the people riot in the arena and in the city and Caracho is forced to disguise himself as a woman to escape from Portugal. Upon his return to Madrid, Rosario, his volatile mistress, cajoles him into promising that the opening fight of the next season will be his last. It is also to be the last for Cairel, who plans to retire to a monastery thereafter. At that fight, however, a ferocious bull jumps from the ring and charges the spectators in the stands. When Caracho leaps into the fray to save them, he succeeds in wounding the bull, but is gored himself. Cairel, who comes to his rescue, is also gored. Both toreadors die as a result of their wounds. After a macabre scene in which Caracho's wife and mistress come to blows over his body, toppling it from its bier to the floor, both toreadors are laid to rest with all the pomp and ceremony the public can afford its heroes.

Only a dauntless humorist like Gómez de la Serna could have created so comically macabre a scene of a death vigil as that described above. Only a paradoxically tragic humorist of Ramón's genius could have written, as concluding lines for the novel, words like the following:

> Finally, they reached the cemetery. The crowd inundated the grounds just as they did the bleachers.
>
> Would all those people fit within those confines? They did and that was the sardonic lesson the cemetery taught them, "You are so few for me!" it showed them, as it swelled miraculously, telling them scornfully at the entrance, "Enter! Enter!"
>
> The toreadors were deposited in niches in that silent patio with something like an arena of death about it . . . dressed in the black and gold toreador's suit of death they were finally taking part in the private bullfight of the cemetery's interminable sabbath . . .[4]

6. La Nardo (The Spikenard), *1930*

Just as Gómez de la Serna had personified Naples in the heroine of a novel written when he was in Madrid, he now, during a sojourn in

Paris, personified Madrid in the heroine of a novel he called *La Nardo*. The title, the name of a fragrant white flower Ramón considered symbolic of Madrid (because it abounds there and because it symbolized for him the white light of Madrid's summertime), is a nickname for the heroine whose pale fairness is an essential element in her embodiment of the city. This novel, rich in costumbristic evocations of Madrid, carries its reader through the Flea Market, the summer street fairs (or *verbenas*) of Madrid, and many of the plazas, streets, and bars of the city. At times, the popular atmosphere is somewhat reminiscent of Galdós' descriptions of the poor sections of Madrid.

In the story, Aurelia (La Nardo), a beautiful young girl, is sent by her aunt to sell cheap goods at a stall in the Flea Market. She is seduced by the worthless Samuel, who takes advantage of her fatalistic attitude before the impending impact of a comet heralding the end of the world, predicted in the newspapers. Planning to profit from her beauty, he takes her to the *verbena,* and circulates her through the bars of Madrid, whetting the appetites of all who see her. A fake "movie producer" dupes them both, and after enjoying Aurelia's favors, disappears. Her downfall, however, has begun. She next picks up a bar "regular," who introduces her to drugs. When this man's family extricates him from this environment, she finds herself alone, but subsequently enters into a liaison with a doctor who comes to her assistance when she faints in the street. To maintain her dependence upon him, he continues to supply her with drugs until he despairs of satisfying her. Her next lovers are Ernesto, a friend of Samuel's, and a wealthy old man who introduces her to orgies. She is by now recognized as a courtesan by all of Madrid. A policeman, noting her resemblance to a rich and inaccessible marquise ardently desired by a wealthy young Venezuelan, introduces her to him. Samuel unexpectedly returns, frightens off the Venezuelan, and, to earn money, enters her in a beauty contest which she wins. One of the contest judges, a respectable old man, falls desperately in love with her. She responds and they live an idyllic passion which causes him to forget his family, position, and obligations. To achieve their desire for eternal union, she suggests they die together and they commit double suicide by a deliberate overdose of drugs.

Passion and death are paralleled throughout this work, as is symbolized at the outset by the dual presentation of the festive *verbena* and the impending catastrophic comet. This duality persists throughout the novel and is climaxed in the final scene when the dying lovers reiterate:

"Only those who die together die beloved."
"Only those who die together die loving one another."
"Only those who know how to die together love forever."[5]

In this novel, more than in *Amber* or in *Aqueduct,* the soul and spirit of the city are personified in the heroine. La Nardo and Madrid merge into one perfectly fused protagonist. To stress this, Ramón invents numerous flattering remarks by Aurelia's lovers indicating their perception of this. This tendency to fuse the locale with his protagonist becomes stronger in Ramón's novels henceforth, as is evinced in both the following works.

7. Las tres gracias (The Three Graces), 1949

In the prelude of this work, Ramón dedicated it to his beloved fellow *madrileños,* and compared it to his other novels about the city, *The Spikenard* and *The Black and White Widow,* saying that he preserved Madrid in this novel.[6] The novel, with its slim thread of a story which serves Ramón as a pretext for writing about Madrid, begins with a general description of the atmosphere of the city and the nature of the *madrileños*. Chapter Two presents a description of the three sisters from whom the title is derived. The next twenty chapters are dedicated to describing the young ladies' jaunts about Madrid, as a pretext for presenting loving verbal descriptions of the parks, plazas, streets, nooks, and hidden corners of Madrid in all seasons. The actual "plot" does not begin until chapter Twenty-three, when Leandro, attracted by all three girls, finally decides to marry Clotilde, the eldest. The basic unimportance of the story is stressed when the preparations for the wedding and the wedding itself are dismissed in one brief line, "Married and moved, they began to live their lives. . . ."[7] A year later, Clotilde dies of bronchial pneumonia. All are distraught, but the second sister, Araceli, proves a great consolation to the widower and he marries her in turn. Very like Clotilde, she seems to combine both the dead wife's traits and her own so that he has the sensation of almost having two wives in one. After a year, she too, dies of pneumonia. The grieving widower then asks his in-laws if he may marry their third daughter, Lola, saying, "Your daughters are for me, the essence and presence of Madrid,"[8] a line, which, basically, expresses the theme and heart of the novel. They object, and Lola herself, to avoid what seems to her almost an incestuous marriage, runs off with her worthless boyfriend, leaving Leandro feeling widowed of all three girls. He grows prematurely old, and spends the rest of his life quietly working and visiting his in-laws, not interested in any other women, because he knows that only with one of these three sisters who personified Madrid could he be happy.

8. Piso bajo (Basement Flat), *1961*

Ramón called this work his "prose poem" of great illusion and restlessness,[9] and he embodied both qualities in its heroine, Olvido. She is the daughter of Don Pedro, a philosopher and professor who abandoned his beautiful wife because of her infidelity and took Olvido, at fourteen, to live with him in a basement flat. She develops into a flirt, takes up with a wild theatrical group living at a hectic pace, and is even arrested with them for disturbing the peace one night when they cause a riot. Frightened by this incident and several other narrow escapes, she settles down somewhat. Her father's only close friend, Hortensio, loves her and asks for her hand. She accepts, but the following day, affected by a dream during the night, she declares her intention, instead, to become a cloistered nun. Her reasoning is that until now her experiences have been incomplete as she has lacked a suitor seeking her hand in marriage. Now, having experienced even this, she can validly weigh alternatives. Olvido enters the convent, her father drinks to alleviate his pain and loneliness, ages rapidly, and eventually dies a lonely death.

In this, as in his previous novels about Madrid, Ramón, whom some critics have compared to Larra and Mesonero Romanos for his costumbristic tendencies, has again succeeded in capturing many facets of Madrid. On its appearance one reviewer commented that Ramón, now more than ever, qualified for the title of Madrid's "superchronicler," the "producer of the most penetrating pages which Madrid has ever merited in literature," adding that Ramón was "not only a doctor of facts about Madrid, but also the inventor of many of them."[10]

B. *Nebulous Novels*

Avant-garde, "gregueristic" writer that he was, Ramón's attempt to produce a new kind of disconnected, fragmentary, and dehumanized novel was to be expected. He fully admitted the deliberate nature of this thrust when he wrote, in 1924, "The first intuition about this kind of book occurred to me when I thought that one cannot read that literature of insistence upon the ordinary, for one should give other consolations to the soul overwhelmed by reality."[11] Much later in life, attempting perhaps to explain his technique in what came to be called his "nebulous novels" *(novelas de la nebulosa),* Ramón wrote, "It seems to me that the lining up of situations and outcomes less and less merits the trouble of being lived and read,"[12] and he explained:

> I am increasingly convinced that to talk sensibly is senseless ... only in the reconstruction of the cerebral "beyond" can one find the meaning of the meaningless.... We are always surprised that the unexpected is not what it seems, but something else, neither better nor worse, but simply *something else....* Our mission is that of sculptors who plastify whatever dreams of reality exist in reality.[13]

In true vanguard fashion, Ramón's dehumanized, puppet-like characters are either equated with things or subservient to them; the traditional structure of a literary work gives way to planned chaos as the intuitive is substituted for the rational; the logical and sequential is replaced by the disconnected and disjuncted, and anecdotes, metaphors, sensations, impressions, and free associations are used with all the license humor and imagination permit to deliberately effect easy transitions from the real to the hallucinatory.

1. El incongruente (The Incongruent One), *1922*

The first of the "nebulous novels" to appear was *The Incongruent One,* a predominantly surrealistic work whose very title indicates that its hero epitomizes the whimsical incongruity so prized by surrealists. Rather than *live* his life, Gustavo, the incongruous hero, born at the opera between acts and distinguished by weird happenings throughout his childhood, early learns to merely let it *happen* to him. So rare and unusual are the Kafkaesque happenings that befall him, as he allows chance and coincidence to rule his life, that he soon loses the ability to distinguish between illusion and reality. His fantasies, in this setting, become highly plausible, and he moves in a whimsically unreal world where time and space seem not to exist and anything can and does happen: pictures change into mirrors when he looks at them, unexpected letters turn up in his pockets, strange lights go on unexpectedly when he enters a room, inanimate objects in store windows come alive and exchange places when he stops to look at them, strange women offer themselves to him; a widow who through an ouija board asks her dead husband's permission to sup, and then to linger with Gustavo, has her first query answered by affirmative taps of the board, her second, by a roaring fire which bursts forth from the table and rapidly burns down the entire apartment house. Even stranger things occur in Gustavo's dreams or in weird dreamlike sequences of happenings characterized by a common incongruence.

Gustavo himself says, "Nothing completely supernatural has ever happened to me. . . . All the jokes destiny has played on me have always had a basis in reality."[14] Throughout this work, Ramón makes frequent use of a technique common in surrealist poetry — the use of litany-like series of unconnected images linked only by subconscious associations.

When Gustavo finally establishes a tie with reality through matrimony (marrying a girl he encountered seated next to him in the cinema after realizing that, incongruously, he and she had been simultaneously watching the movie and starring in it on the screen), he loses his incongruity.

This novel, with its theme of incongruity, is one of the least coherent written by Ramón. His subsequent "nebulous" novels follow more traceable themes and have, consequently, a greater measure of coherence.

2. El novelista (The Novelist), *1923*

Although not nearly as "nebulous" as the former novel, Ramón includes this work among his "nebulous novels," possibly because of the enormous richness and creativity of its thematic variety. It is the story of Andrés, a novelist in the process of proofreading a new edition of his largely biographical novel, "La apasionada." Much parallels Gómez de la Serna's life in this novel, as the author seems to step back from himself and point out to his readers his own characteristics, his creative processes, and attitudes. Like himself, Ramón's novelist writes several novels simultaneously, refuses the distraction of visitors, and sometimes walks the streets seeking people with forms and faces suitable for his characters. The novel includes scenes in which his author's callers sometimes insist upon seeing him, convinced that they are characters from his books, even though he never met them before publishing his works. Like Ramón, Andrés goes to Paris, London, and Lisbon seeking inspiration. Ramón inserts several excellent embryonic plots in the novel, about Siamese twins, for example, or about a doctor who had fathered twins and concealed the existence of the second child, reserving him for use in scientific experiments such as an artificial heart transplant. None of these highly imaginative plot outlines appears elsewhere in Ramón's works. Despite its enormous thematic variety, however, *The Novelist* shows a relative absence of evolution in Ramón's style and content.

3. El hombre perdido (The Lost Man), *1924*

Greater incoherence and lack of continuity in the loose episodes or amplified *greguerías* which revolve about the protagonist characterize Gómez de la Serna's third "nebulous novel." Ramón explains the nature of this work and its protagonist in the prologue when he writes, "Life and death are an illusion, the illusion of finding oneself," and tells us that here he collects "something of the chaos of our era — which probably has been the chaos of always."[15] His lost man, he tells us, is one of an innumerable multitude of men who have deliberately chosen not to believe in the conventional, the sordid, the regular and ordered aspects of life, but preferred its formless, even its illusory qualities.

The "lost" protagonist of this novel is an unlikely character to whom unlikely things happen, a nameless man who suffers from a feeling of guilt for some forgotten crime committed in a past generation, the remembrance of which would help him to establish his identity. The work is a mixture of fantasy and memory, frequently tinged with the erotic. Its nebulous subject has no friends, no relatives, no home. He sustains disconnected, unrelated conversations with other "nebulous" people, confessing that he feels lost because he has not found himself, yet adding that the greatest farce in life is really to believe that one is who he thinks he is. Feeling very much a traveler through life, he is, nevertheless, anxious to find his destiny. Inanimate things speak to him and a series of erotic adventures befall him with women he meets purely by chance in shops, on trains, or who call to him from balconies or doorways when he goes by. At one point, his imaginings become so highly erotic that he even believes himself in love with the bathroom fixtures:

I began to love the bathroom sink, its aseptic porcelain, its shiny faucets, the combination of its clean basin with the moonlike shine of its porcelain and the rustless fidelity of its tubing. Had I been able to say so, I would have declared, "I have fallen in love with the porcelain muscles of my washbowl, with the spigot which, responding to my hand lets me turn the water on and off at will.[16]

In the end, tired and alone, avoiding the comfortable life he might have attained through marriage with a rich woman, he simply lies down on a railroad track and is run over by a train. Next day, the newspaper carries this brief item: "In the public lands bordering the railway system in the south, a man's cadaver was found. The body was so mutilated that it was impossible to identify."[17] The "lost" protagonist remains nameless, in life and in death. He is, from beginning to end, simply *un hombre perdido,* a lost man.

The continuous pointless chain of transitory, insignificant happenings which befall the protagonist explains his despair at the emptiness of life and his desperate search for a more meaningful reality than the superficially apparent one. He goes through life seeking "to encounter something convincing that assures us of having lived,"[18] but his search is unavailing and the meaning of life and the ultimate reality continue to elude him.

This work abounds in instances of surrealistic humor and chaotic passages in which dreams, fantasies, and reality are counterpoised and intermingled, resulting in strange sequences of almost lyric quality.

4. !Rebeca! *(1936)*

*Ramo*n considered ¡*Rebeca!* his first completely nebulous novel. Its surrealistic hero, Luís (who has no surname), tired of his relatives' persistent questioning about his lady friends, one day answers their questions by spontaneously inventing an imaginary sweetheart whom he names Rebeca and whom he even endows with a physical description. Then, having created the concept of Rebeca, he becomes obsessed by it and "she" becomes for him the embodiment of perfect happiness. He seeks Rebeca, or facets of her, everywhere, imagining her-him-it with him frequently and engages in long non sequitur conversations with her. He sees Rebeca variously in a teapot, as the whitecap on an ocean wave, as a picture in a museum, and so on. As his obsession grows, he even writes and mails letters to her at an invented address, and though he makes love to numerous women, they are all merely Rebeca substitutes. People begin to ridicule him and to send him anonymous letters from or about Rebeca. Once he is shocked to encounter a tombstone in a cemetery marked "Rebeca," and on another occasion, after reading in the newspaper about a murdered woman named Rebeca, he is arrested on suspicion of murder when he goes to view her corpse at the morgue. Rebeca becomes a symbol of all he seeks in life, and he even advises a friend,

"I have Rebeca. Find yourself another symbol."[19] Once Rebeca appears to him in a dream as the embodiment of revolution. This curious incident, written prior to the book's publication in 1936, reflects Ramón's forebodings about the impending Civil War. It is unusual in Ramón because politics never directly entered into his works. In this one highly unusual scene, he totally rejects the feminine embodiment of revolution, saying, "As soon as I hear you come, I shall be your fugitive."[20] Finally, however, when he all but despairs of ever encountering his Rebeca, he is introduced to a Jewish woman at a reception. She seems to truly understand him, and, realizing that in her he has found the only attainable Rebeca, he marries her.

This novel, with its patently autobiographical aspects, surrealistic sequences, weird, unconnected conversations and episodes, confusion of reality and fantasy, formlessness and lack of cohesion and continuity, marks the end of Ramón's deliberately nebulous novels and the end of the early, relatively carefree period of his life.

Besides these works of ambient and nebulous surreality, Ramón wrote at least six other full-length "novels." Although they all display a wide variety of plot and theme, they are basically ramonesque in their loosely joined, anecdotal construction and unattached, bohemian type heroes.

C. *Anecdotal Novels*

1. El doctor inverosímil (The Unlikely Doctor), *1914*

The earliest of the anecdotal novels, *The Unlikely Doctor* has no plot at all. Ramón doesn't even name the doctor (Vivar) until the sixth chapter. He seems merely to enjoy writing his variations on the theme of unlikely, whimsical cases and to indulge his imagination with them. Vivar is a Sherlock Holmes type doctor, stalking the source of his patients' strange illnesses and finding them, for example, in the old leather gloves one patient wears, whose secretions of past experiences make him ill; in the contamination of "suicide infection" a fellow doctor received from a patient; in the obsessive recollection of a nude woman which affects the heart of a highly susceptible young man; in the glare of lights which upsets a young lady at parties; and in the poisonous air one patient unwittingly imbibes from a collection of old pipes, like old sick throats exhaling constantly about him. Ramón uses the term "allergies" and has his unlikely doctor prescribe minute doses of the irritant to build up resistance against it. Other cases include a cavalry soldier allergic to horses, a young woman allergic to sardines, an actor allergic to stage makeup; there are allergies to roses, white wine, metal odor, velvet, perfume, guinea pigs, Havana cigars, weeds, butterflies, dust, and even plaster-of-Paris.

This arbitrary succession of unusual cases is generally resolved by one of the doctor's "superscientific" flashes of insight. Ramón seems to be hinting, perhaps unwittingly, at instances of what has come to be known as "psychosomatic medicine."

2. El Gran Hotel (Grand Hotel), *1922*

In *Grand Hotel,* Manuel Quevedo, a young man who receives a modest inheritance, decides to use it by living in luxury as long as it lasts. He goes to Geneva to stay at the luxurious Grand Hotel until his money is exhausted. There, he is frustrated by his lack of success in feminine conquests (although he had always been successful previously in the second- or third-class hotels he had frequented). When he acquires a young prostitute companion, he is upset when she leaves him after a very brief liaison. After that he accosts an attractive young woman guest on the stairs, but is abruptly repulsed. Then he becomes the lover of a young Cuban guest, only to discover that she is having a last fling before being admitted to a nearby tuberculosis sanitarium. Finally a Russian countess arrives, whose very presence lends distinction to the hotel. Quevedo is not long in discovering that she will favor whoever pays her lavish expenses. This is the kind of woman and affair he had dreamed of. Olimpia frequently dresses in classic white, and always has an inimitable elegance. He falls so sincerely in love with her, that he even proposes marriage, but she merely laughs at the thought of a bourgeois married life. Although he is disappointed, he realizes it is for the best. Already his money is running out and his days are numbered. On the day of his departure, he tips everyone generously so that he will be remembered and sets out for Madrid. As he settles back on the train, he wryly notes the sign below the window reading, "It is dangerous to look out the window."

The novel includes numerous vignettes about luxury living in an expensive hotel and about the cross-section of human types passing through it. It is more cohesive than most of Ramón's novels in structure and plot, and remains consistently light and humorous in mood, even in the somewhat unramonesque scenes of sadness, illness, or egotism which occasionally mar the perfection of the protagonist's luxurious escapade.

3. El chalet de las rosas (The Chalet of the Roses), *1926*

In this variation of the Bluebeard theme, Don Roberto Gascón, a suave old bachelor, subtly seduces with promises of marriage a series of three lonely, maturing women, whom he singles out in such places as parks, train stations, or restaurants. He takes each one to live in his "Chalet of the Roses," a charming little villa on the outskirts of the city and encourages each to withdraw her savings or pension funds and turn them over to him for "investment," whereupon he appropriates the capital while giving her "interest." As he tires of each one, he calmly eliminates her, appropriates her jewels, and buries her corpse by night in his rose garden. When he learns that his third victim has fallen heir to a modest fortune, he persuades Amanda, his fourth mistress, to feign her identity and claim it. Thereafter, Amanda becomes increasingly suspicious of him. They escape to Paris where he studies taxidermy and eventually confesses his secret to a mysterious friend, Kroztia. When he falls in love with Kroztia's "ward," Amanda, jealous and apprehensive, tells the police her suspicions regarding his previous "wives." They arrest him, investigate, find the bodies, and condemn him to death by hanging.

Although a number of Ramón's short stories might be classified as "mysteries" or "detective" stories, this is his only full-length novel of that nature. Nevertheless, his Bluebeard, created with a typically ramonesque touch of whimsical humor, is a gentlemanly and refined assassin; a calm perfectionist who prides himself on each "task" well done; a charming old gentleman who is a little more culpable, but no less delightful than the gracious protagonists of *Arsenic and Old Lace*. Unlike them, however, his crimes are not motivated by kindly intentions, but by a mixture of avarice, sexual desire, and egoism. Appropriately, therefore, his end is a harsher one.

3. Cinelandia (Movieland), *1927*

In *Movieland* Ramón presents his concept of Hollywood. Countless movie character "types" pass through the novel: thrill seekers, bad men, fat men, background men, child prodigies, ingenues, screen lovers, starlets, playboys, avaricious directors and drunks, but it has no true protagonist. It is the ambient, with its incessant gossip, inane cocktail parties, promiscuity, obsession with sex, and so on, which is the novel's true protagonist. Ramón imitates cinematic techniques and depicts movieland in kaleidoscopic, fragmentary glimpses and disconnected chapters. Despite his intention to present the potpourri of "Movieland," the novel doesn't quite come off, for Ramón was writing about something he knew nothing about. The novel is not convincing; and, in its striving for effect, falls short of Ramón's usual high imaginative level. It has no plot or conclusion and seems merely to play with its subject, rather than to really penetrate or project it.

4. El Caballero del hongo gris (The Gentleman in the Grey Top Hat), *1928*

When Leonardo, the protagonist, acquires a grey top hat, which gives him "presence," he becomes so audaciously self-confident he feels he can do anything. He becomes an impresario, an entrepreneur, a confidence man, always successful in whatever he undertakes. When, however, he meets a stranger wearing a similar grey top hat, he feels threatened, loses his self-confidence, and quits.

Ramón uses Leonardo as a linking thread for a series of audaciously amusing escapades. The narrative is never serious or moralizing and the cause of the hero's eventual retirement from the active scene is as farcically humorous as the rest of the narrative.

5. Policéfalo y señora (Polycephalous and Wife), *1932*

Perfecto Tully is, as his name indicates, a polycephalous, or many-headed hero. As pictured by Ramón, he has a typically Argentine, cosmopolitan heritage which somewhat exaggeratedly includes Spanish, Burmese, Norwegian, Irish, Russian, Venetian, Mexican, and Portuguese forebears. He marries Edma, the daughter of a wealthy landowner whose forebears are Spanish, English, Chinese and French. They are two disparate beings, in accord only on their wedding night. On their honeymoon trip to Europe, they are surprised to find that they react to the different environment of each country by involuntarily bringing to the surface characteristics inherited from their forebears from that country. They become increasingly ·incompatible, and eventually agree to a divorce. Subsequently, after a series of affairs, Perfecto falls in love with Nadina whom he meets when his car runs into her shortly after he has traded cars (and consequently destinies) with an acquaintance. By dint of denying him nothing, Nadina (whose name *means* "nothing") comes, paradoxically, to rule him completely. To save himself from her domination, he leaves Nadina when he returns to Argentina to claim the inheritance willed him by his father. To effect this return, he hires a plane for a then unheard-of direct flight from Paris to Buenos Aires.

In this episodic work, Ramón seems to have been amusing himself by playing with the notoriously multinational background of the Argentines, as if engaged in an elaborate practical joke. He even headed the chapters in this novel with nonsense titles, such as "LSLSLSLSLS," "¿STS?" or "OXINXIIS EOLTMRA." Perfecto and Edma, like Ramón's other vagabond characters, serve merely as connecting links between anecdotes.

CHAPTER 4

Fiction: Novelettes, "Superhistorical" Novels

I Novelettes

BECAUSE Gómez de la Serna's short novels are so numerous (and often difficult to find), they are arranged here not by order of their individual chronological appearance, but rather according to the chronological appearance of the more easily accessible collections in which they were subsequently published. Wherever possible the date of each story's original appearance is indicated in parenthesis after its title. Five novelettes, published independently and not subsequently included in such collections, are treated separately after the collections. Like Ramón's dramas, many of these "short novels" first appeared in magazines like *Promoteo* or *Revista de Occidente;* others were published separately in limited, cheap editions. Like his plays, too, these works are highly imaginative, ingenious, and varied; they are precipitous little works that could not have been sustained for an extended number of pages, but which, in their brevity, serve as perfect vehicles for the sprightly wit and ingenuity of their author.

A. La malicia de las acacias (The Malice of the Acacia Flowers, *1924. Collection)*

This volume, Ramón's first collection of short novels, contains the following nine stories.

1. "The Malice of the Acacia Flowers" (1923) is a story about Filo and Flora who meet when his dog chases her in the park; subsequently they become sweethearts. When a friend of theirs dies from typhus, Filo pursuades Flora to yield to him, rationalizing that they should not die unfulfilled, as did their friend. Flora becomes pregnant and deliberately aborts the child, giving Filo the newspaper-

wrapped embryo to dispose of. He does this by tying a stone to the package and dropping it into a lake. Their crime unites them even more. Although Filo doesn't yet feel ready to marry and plans to stop seeing Flora, he fears to do so lest she denounce him. Moreover, he realizes that, being accomplices, they cannot separate.

When they eventually marry, their one desire is to have a son, as if thereby they can compensate for the lost one. Inadvertently, however, Flora aborts again. Brokenhearted, they plan an elaborate funeral with coach and horses, wreaths, a niche for the fetus, and so on. Everyone is surprised at this excessive display of grief, not realizing that Filo and Flora need this catharsis for their past guilt.

2. "Los gemelos y el guante" ("The Opera Glasses and the Glove"). Clemente met Encarnación at a masked ball where earlier his friend Carrasco had flirted unsuccessfully with her. When they married, their first year together was difficult for, obsessed by the idea that she looked down on him, he tried in vain to dominate her.

One evening, in reconciliation after a quarrel, he takes her to the opera. Her beauty attracts all eyes and he is proud of her. When she gazes around the theater through her opera glasses, however, he notices Carrasco, looking back at her, and assumes that they are exchanging glances through their opera glasses. During the intermission he seeks out Carrasco in the lobby and, in the presence of Carrasco's friends, throws a glove in his face, challenging him to a duel. That night, after putting his wife tenderly to bed, he goes out to duel with Carrasco and is killed. Everyone is appalled, for no one really wanted to kill anyone, and they decide to take him home saying he was run over by a car.

3. "El joven de las sobremeas" ("The After-dinner Guest"). Don Santiago is a nightly after-supper guest or *tertuliano* of Mateo and Dora. They all enjoy one another's company and pass long evenings pleasantly chatting and playing the gramophone.

When their neighbors in the small town become envious and begin to harass them with anonymous notes, the three begin to feel a little uncomfortable at their *tertulias*. Finally, Dora realizes that the most frequent sender of the anonymous letters must be a woman in love with Santiago. Upon comparing their letters, they realize that they are all made of words and letters cut from the *El Sol* newspaper. Santiago investigates and learns that, along the route he travels to his friend's home, the only regular subscriber to *El Sol* is indeed a woman. Curious, he begins pausing at her window and chatting with her en route to his friends' home. As he becomes increasingly interested in her, their chats become longer and longer, until finally, conquered by the lady en route, he no longer arrives at Mateo's home.

4. "La Tormenta" ("The Storm"). Rubén, an adolescent, learns the facts of life from his friend, Manuel. Thereafter, he becomes aware of the budding womanhood of Elvira, the orphan cousin, approximately his age, whom his parents are raising. One day, he returns from school to find his parents out. Alone with Elvira when she is made nervous by a summer storm, he coaxes her to sit by him on the sofa, and then embraces, kisses, and makes love to her.

Ramón concludes this story on a moralizing note unusual for him, saying, "He will marry young and have many children.... he will ... be mediocre and ... a failure all his life."[1] Although Ramón's portrayal of adolescent curiosity and experimentation is sensitive and perceptive, his unexpected final admonishment is incongruously out of keeping here.

5. "La Gallipava" ("The Turkey-Hen"). Señor Rebazo loves and humors his wife, and because she doesn't like their dark apartment, he builds a two-room house for her in a nearby small town. There, however, she finds herself bored and lonesome and decides to take up gardening. Always excessive, she plants so thickly that nothing grows. Discouraged, she turns to raising chickens. She succeeds in this, and becomes as attached to her brood as if they were children, pointing out to Rebazo each one's individual characteristics and idiosyncrasies. When a hen begins to lay her daily egg in the middle of their bed, however, he irately demands she keep the chickens out of their house, and angrily calls her "Gallipava" (Turkey-hen). The name sticks and others use it. Gradually she seems to take on the characteristics of a chicken, cocking her head to one side and looking sideways instead of turning her eyes, to see laterally. People, knowing her mania, jest about it.

Upset by these mannerisms, Rebazo takes his wife to a doctor, who discovers that she cocks her head to one side to see laterally because one eye is paralyzed. Repentent, he apologizes for calling her "Gallipava," and for the rest of his life regrets having thoughtlessly given her a derisive nickname because of a handicap beyond her control.

6. "Miedo al mar" ("Fear of the Sea"). Sagrario, worried because of her boyfriend Prudencio's unreasonable fear of the sea, mentions it to her family doctor who says that Prudencio may have "pelagra." This is a fatal seasickness whose victims are fascinated by the sea to the point where they unite with it and drown; its tell tale sign is a rosy hue on the hands. That evening when they are with friends, she observes that his hands are normal in color, but that her friend, Asunción, has rosy-hued hands. She had known of Asunción's fascination with the sea. Now that she comprehends it, Sagrario resolves to accompany her friend constantly to prevent her drowning. Eventually Sagrario's ever-closer friendship with Asunción offends Prudencio, and he leaves her.

It seems as if Ramón here, toying with the concept of "seasickness," wrote a fantasy story based largely on its whimsically literal interpretation.

7. "De otra raza" ("Of Another Race"). This story is based on the theme of internal struggle caused by mixed bloods. Don Emilio Calvaro, who has worked relentlessly in the Philippines to accumulate money for a comfortable retirement in Madrid, finally returns there with his Philippine wife, his son, Vicente, whose Philippine-Chinese features resemble his mother's, and his daughter, Dulce Nombre, whose Spanish features resemble his.

Vicente makes only one good friend in Madrid, the slightly hump-backed Wences. At carnival time, when Vicente, dressed as a Chinese warrior, fails to win the masquerade contest, loses track of his friend Wences during the carnival, and misses the romantic adventures he had anticipated, he is frustrated. Arriving home in the closing hours of the carnival in time to see his sister (whom he secretly envies and hates) parting from a masked figure whom he recognizes as Wences, he is furious that even Wences prefers her to him! He follows his sister inside, berating her. When she angrily shouts back, calling him "Chino," he takes the short sword from his warrior costume and slits her throat.

A maid, attracted by the noise, runs screaming from the scene to tell their parents. The mother struggles with her irate husband to keep him from killing Vicente, and the story concludes: "The other race shone in him, victorious and sublime."[2]

8. "La Gangosa" ("The Woman With the Twangy Voice"). Rafael, a regular customer at the Mallorquina tea room hears

Regina's twangy voice as she sits at a nearby table with her mother and sister. Regina flirts with him and, when they leave, he follows her to see where she lives. He eventually manages to meet, court, and marry her. They are happy until someone informs him that he'd seen Regina at the Palace Cafe recently. Suspicious, he wonders if she is seeing another man, and begins to frequent the Cafe watching for her. There, he meets and begins an affair with another woman. When they go to any cafes he always carefully sits facing the door. Finally, one day he sees Regina look in and retreat hurriedly upon seeing him. He hurries home to confront her, telling her accusingly that a man came in shortly behind her, looked about as if seeking her, and left. Relaxed and languid as ever, Regina asks what he was doing in the cafe. Realizing that she probably saw him with his lady friend, he backs down. Regina promises that she will stay at home in the future if he will do the same. He agrees and thereafter they are closer than before.

9. "Aquella novela" ("That Novel"). Esteban returns to the Luxembourg gardens where, on his last trip to Paris, he had initiated a romantic adventure with an attractive divorcee. This time he sees a young girl, Matilde, sitting on a bench, reading. Upon seeing him she smiles. He joins her, chats, and ends up taking her to a hotel where she readily yields to him after informing him, *Je suis vierge* ("I am a virgin").

They meet daily, thereafter. He both doubts and believes her statement, unable to understand why she was both so innocent and so accessible. At the theater one night, she greets a friend whom he insists join them, hoping to question him later. The man, a lifelong friend of hers, verifies that she is a young woman of integrity and good family.

Esteban becomes obsessed with solving the mystery of her easy surrender. Finally it occurs to him to ask what book she was reading the day he met her. Embarrassed, she tells him *El perfume indiscreto,* by Lorine. He reads the book and realizes that *it* had rendered her susceptible to his advances and that the same thing would have happened regardless of who came along. Although he is disillusioned, he feels free, realizing that he is not to blame for her yielding, and consequently, owes her nothing. He packs and leaves Paris with great relief. As his train pulls away, he begins rereading the novel reinforcing his sense of justification in leaving her.

B. Seis falsas novelas (Six Pseudo Novels), *1927. (Collection*

Fiction: Novelettes

Almost as an exercise in versatility, Ramón set himself the task of writing a series of pseudonational or regional stories, trusting to the accumulated recollections and subconscious impressions he had acquired through his wide reading to imbue his parodies with an aura of authenticity. Two of the stories first appeared like trial balloons in 1925, and the collection of six tales entitled *Seis falsas novelas (Six Pseudo Novels)* followed in 1927. Many years and editions later, in the prologue to the 1945 edition, Ramón proudly labeled his pseudo novels "a new genre,"[3] and attributed their success to their basic simplicity and to "miracles of the subconscious." As in the "superhistorical" novels published later in 1944, these parodies so skillfully combine an aura of authenticity with subjective, creative fantasy that they have a large element of the poetic. Although they vary in length from fourteen to thirty pages, Ramón calls them all "novels" rather than "stories," a fact which adds to the confusion in organizing his works.

1. "María Yarsilovna," a pseudo-Russian novel, was written, Ramón tells us, out of his nostalgia for old Russian novels and his desire to produce "the final unpublished Russian novel of the past."[4] It is the story of a foreigner in Russia, who falls in love with María Yarsilovna, the beautiful daughter of his neighbor, Fedor. Her pale, cool, and controlled beauty reminds him of a wan or sleeping princess and her reserved silence intrigues him.

One evening, when he is invited to Fedor's home, the other guests speak of "Prince Hich" who is soon to return among them, ordained a priest. At the subsequent gathering, Hich, looking very princely despite his priestly robes, arrives. María seems paler than ever, and later that evening her voice is heard screaming from the rear of the house that she is dying. Everyone races to her assistance and when she begs for absolution, all but Hich leave. After an unduly long time, he returns to the group, bringing a transformed María by the hand. Her pale remoteness is replaced by a rosy, bourgeois, almost housewifely glow. Her aloofness gone, the stranger is no longer attracted to her, for she now seems merely ordinary to him.

In this, as in many of his novels, Ramón has chosen to embody the ambient in the person of his female protagonist by personifying the remote coldness of Russia in María. Ramón, the idealist, shows here that when the exotic loses its remoteness, it also loses its charm.

2. In "Los dos marineros" ("The Two Sailors"), Ramón has produced a pseudo-Chinese novel. In it Niquita, a lovely Chinese

girl, deceived by her sailor-lover Yama, turns for consolation to Nachauri, a lake sailor. When a fortune-teller warns her of impending danger, Niquita visits nearby shrines and decorates them with flowers in the hope of forestalling disaster. One night, as the lovers sleep, Yama, sword in hand, breaks into their hut and attacks Nachauri. Nachauri, unarmed but cool, wrestles Yama's clean and shining sword from him, and kills him with it.

Although this story has numerous incidental Chinese details such as slant eyes, bamboo huts, Buddhist shrines, and brooding oriental mystery and vengeance, its simple plot of primitive passion and revenge and its final scene of violence never succeed in seeming anything but pseudo-Chinese.

3. "La Fúnebre" ("The Fatal Lady"), Ramón's false Tartar novel, was first published independently in 1925, perhaps as a sort of trial balloon, perhaps as a lucky stroke. Its success gave rise to the idea of the subsequent series. This story takes place in the village of Kikir, in the land of the Tartars, where there lived a young woman whose neighbors called her "the fatal one" because her six successive husbands had followed one another to an early death, shortly after marriage. After Kikir's strongest man becomes the seventh victim, the intrepid Tubal accepts the challenge of becoming number eight. At the wedding, so apprehensive are the guests that they scarcely know whether to express sentiments of joy or commiseration. Everyone, including Tubal and his new wife, nervously anticipates the inevitable fate. Finally, unable to bear the suspense any longer, Tubal decides that if he is to be victor rather than victim, he must take the initiative. One night, while his unsuspecting wife lies sleeping at his side, he takes his sword in hand and as a premeditated measure of self-defense cleanly slits her throat.

Ramón concludes this short novel with the morbid comment that, although Tubal breathed freely after his act, believing death quite distant, it is in reality, "never far away and one is always number so and so among the spouses of life."[5]

4. "La virgen pintada de rojo" ("The Virgin Painted Red"), a pseudo-black novel, was also first published in 1925. In this story, a nubile, black adolescent beauty, Luma, the pride of the village of Motombo, is desired by all the men who come from far and near to see her. According to custom, when she reaches puberty, she will be won in a race of fair pursuit in which the youth who overtakes her

Fiction: Novelettes [69]

wins the right to marry her. When the day arrives, Luma is painted red, according to custom, by the old women of the village. Her six major pursuers employ various strategies of guile or cunning in their attempts to win her, and Bauziri even prays to the devil for help. In the race, Luma, tired and frightened, cries out his name. Bauziri hears her and answers. When he reaches and assaults her, they exchange no kisses, for kisses, Ramón explains, have not yet been discovered. After their initial passion cools and they rest, Luma follows him docilely back to town, thereby proclaiming their marriage. When two months' retirement have passed (as required by tribal custom), she will be allowed to sit in his cabin doorway and smoke her pipe, like the other married women of Motombo.

Ramón's somewhat stereotyped concept of African life, primitive cunning, tribal customs, taboos, and mating rituals, is rich in picturesque detail. In the prologue of a 1945 edition of this work, he notes proudly that when this story was read over the radio in Germany, an expert on African folklore commented that he had never heard a more exact description of the vegetation and customs of those torrid lands than in this story. Ramón attributes this to the miraculous powers of the subconscious. The "African expert" remains nameless, however, and his authenticity may well be as dubious as that of the novel his testimony "authenticates."

5. "La mujer vestida de hombre" ("The Woman Who Dressed Like a Man") is a pseudo-German novel, about Marien, a lovely twenty-two-year-old who, unable to attract masculine attention with her purely feminine charms, decides, instead, to challenge the opposite sex by adopting masculine attire. Her bobbed hair, slim suit-clad figure, walking stick, and long-stemmed cigarette holder arouse attention wherever she goes and eventually succeed in awakening the interest of her brother's friend, Otto. Her attire also liberates her from the usual feminine conventions, enabling her to walk freely through the streets and even to enter bars and cabarets unescorted.

A movie director sees in her the prototype of the contemporary woman and offers to make a star of her. In the end, her dress prevails upon her personality, and, rather than leave the movie studio and return to the outside world (which she fears would only attempt to reduce her to the traditional female role), she elects to remain at the studio, consecrating herself entirely to her vocation as the modern woman.

Ramón's anticipation of today's feminine liberation movement is as curious here as is his anticipation of the practice of psychosomatic medicine and the splitting of the atom in other works.

6. "El hijo del millonario" ("The Millionaire's Son") is a psuedo-North American novel. In it, David Karvaler, son of a New York millionaire, likes fast cars and dangerous kicks — like running over people in his car and leaving them dead in the road; cutting off the ears of prostitutes for his jarred collection, or dressing as a Ku Klux Klanner to frighten the entire Negro audience out of a theater. Death fascinates him, and he courts it by inciting a patron to stab an innkeeper, by paying an Oriental to commit hari-kari in his presence so he can observe the ritual, and finally, by constructing a windowless factory in which two thousand workmen die when an explosion sets the building aflame. Subsequent investigation reveals his guilt and brings his collection of severed ears to light. Unions and earless ladies alike demand his life. When he is electrocuted, death surprises him in the act of putting on a monocle. Ramón concludes this story with the morbid observation that death frequently surprises its victims in an unfinished act; to await its conclusion would be an affectation.

It is interesting that Ramón chose to use the hot-rodding thrill-seeking son of a wealthy industrialist as the protagonist for his pseudo-North American novel. The grotesquely criminal bent of the pampered young millionaire is a typically ramonesque twist of plot and fancy.

C. El dueño del átomo (The Master of the Atom), *1928. (Collection)*

The nine stories included in this collection, ranging in tone from the sheerly fantastic to the sensuous and almost realistic, provide an excellent sampling of Ramón's work.

1. "El dueño del átomo" ("The Master of the Atom"), 1928. Don Alfredo, a researcher in an obscure institute, promises his sweetheart Angela that they will become rich when he achieves his goal of splitting the atom. They marry and live a quiet life except for a few regular dinner guests: a colleague, an old schoolmate, and a favored student.

Alfredo becomes so obsessed with his experiment that he ages unduly. Angela, hoping for riches, encourages him. When he senses success, he sends for her to witness his great experiment and then begins. Instantly, without noise or noticeable cause, the wall before

Fiction: Novelettes

them and all successive walls disintegrate; the street, the church and church tower crumble and still the force cannot be halted. Finally, in desperation, Don Alfredo breaks the tube behind them and "the halved microelectron drew back upon feeling the magnetism of its other half, invaded a new sector of dissolution, and made the three astonished onlookers invisible."[6]

In this story Ramón, for once, has not written a superfluous word. The abrupt ending befits the characters' final and complete "disappearance." The buildup of suspense comprises most of the story, and the climax occurs on the final page in eight very brief paragraphs. Ramón needs no long, playful, verbal passages here. The plot itself is so humorously effective that it needs no embellishment. The brevity of the work contributes to its impact and to the humor of its surprise ending.

2. "La casa triangular" ("The Triangular House"). Adolfo Sureda, hoping to build a completely "different" house for his bride, hired an architect who helped him build a triangular house which even contained some triangular furniture. One day he encountered a geometrician outside his house busily making calculations about it. They became friends and the geometrician began to teach Adolfo geometry so that he could discuss his house with greater confidence. One day, Adolfo received an anonymous letter informing him that his wife was having an affair. He consulted the geometrician, who, using equations, showed him that he was point "B" of an isosceles triangle and his wife was angle "A"; since "C" had to equal "A," "C" must be a close relative who frequented the house. Adolfo, realizing that his wife's first cousin did in fact frequent the house, stormed into her room, shouting accusingly, "So, it's Enrique?" Frightened, she asked how he knew, thereby giving herself away. They separated that same day and he placed a triangular sign on the triangular house saying, somewhat squarely, "For Sale."

3. "El Ruso" ("The Russian") is a Russian restaurant in Paris which Ramón frequented. While dining alone there, he enjoyed observing the other diners, especially women, and even fantasied about some of the habituées. Finally, he settled his attentions on Paulowa, sharing her table silently at first, then, eventually, engaging her in conversation. She told him of her loneliness for her husband, Sergio, condemned to Siberia, and showed him the good-looking, strong exile's picture. Impressed by her dignity, Ramón resolved to remain correct and respectfully attentive in his manner to her.

When the time came for him to leave Paris, she seemed sad to say good-bye and he wondered if perhaps she might not have been willing to establish a liaison. Could he have missed his chance? Tardily, he eyed the other habituées of the restaurant and regretted that he had not spent his time where it might have resulted in romance.

4. "El gran griposo" ("The Great Grippe Victim") tells the story of Antonio Rojas, who suffers repeatedly from attacks of influenza, consults numerous doctors, friends and acquaintances, and tries countless remedies, all to no avail as he continues to endure progressively worse attacks of grippe. Through his protagonist, Ramón here literally plays with the idea of the flu, perceiving it in various ways, and even personifying it as a woman with whom he comes to feel almost married, so inseparable is it from him. Finally, as he had feared, the grippe totally absorbs him and he dies of it.

One wonders if perhaps Ramón might not have written this story while or shortly after suffering an attack of influenza himself.

5. "La hija del verano" ("The Daughter of Summer") concerns the adolescent Adelaida, who, with the beginning of summer, reaches the first fresh bloom of radiant young womanhood. Each day as summer progresses, she blossoms more. Miguel promises his friends that he will be the first to savor her fresh full ripeness and he succeeds in seducing her. Their idyllic passion is subsequently marred by her regrets and recriminations when he refuses to marry her, precisely because of the head-turning quality of sensuous beauty which had attracted him. He breaks off with her, and a few months later she marries a relative. Ramón concludes this tale with the observation that the remembrance of that summer will remain indelibly in Miguel's mind, for in life there is only one such moment of luscious ripeness, ardor, and passion.

6. "Hombre de la galería" ("The Man in the Gallery"). In a melancholy little inner gallery of shops, off a main street in Naples, Don Giovanni Mormoso customarily strolled each afternoon, looking at the shop windows, the displays, the passersby, the street lamps, the birds, and benches — all that comprised the peaceful familiarity this little corner of the world held for him. Each day he dressed carefully and once a week he tinted his hair, so that he always looked elegant during his promenades through the gallery. Sometimes he chatted with the shop-people, but generally he preferred to be alone.

When a blind man who frequented the gallery imposed his company too much upon him, he denounced him to the police for begging, and so rid himself of his unwelcome company. One day, however, the lamp of a street light in the gallery fell squarely upon his head, killing him on the spot.

Ramón concludes whimsically that the fatal blow seemed suspiciously premeditated, for Don Giovanni had passed beneath that particular street lamp too many times not to be recognized by it.

7. "La saturada" ("The Sated One"). Salvador, a bachelor of about forty who lived with his sister, was strongly attracted to his seventeen-year-old niece. The girl, headstrong and unrestrained, went out every night with a succession of boyfriends and gave herself freely to any and all of them. Salvador waited patiently for her to reach a saturation point so that he could offer her true love and marry her without risking her possible restlessness and infidelity later. His long, patient wait sometimes seemed hopeless, for her radiant beauty and exuberance were never spent. One night during carnival, he decided to escort her and found her childlike insatiability appalling. She ate and drank monstrously, insisted upon going to the Circus Theater where she shrieked, laughed uproariously, and even volunteered to assist the magician and the lion tamers with their tricks, thereby attracting the attention of the entire audience. His embarrassment was deepened by having seen some acquaintances and friends in the theater. When she challenged him to culminate the evening's activities, he backed off, saying that he had merely wanted to take her out as he had when she was a child, indulging her whims. Irrepressible and undaunted, she thanked him and breezily left to join her friends. He returned home tired and discouraged, realizing at last that she would never be sated and willing to settle down with him, for she was voraciously insatiable.

8. "El olor de las mimosas" ("The Fragrance of the Mimosas"). The narrator, a young electrical engineer of marriageable age vacationing in a small town, singles out two of the town's eligible young women for consideration. When Paz, the first, proves to be too aggressive and demanding, he concentrates his attention on the second, the more modest and simple Adelaida. In early summer, she blossoms apace with the mimosa flowers, but as summer draws to an end, like them, she becomes paler and seems almost to age and wither. When she tells him that her room has twin beds, he feels

repulsed, as if she were planning to trap him into the extra bed, or as if it had been vacated by someone now dead. He seeks a pretext for arguing with her and then leaves on the next train, escaping from the marriage she had too eagerly projected.

Just as Ramón personified cities in the protagonists of some of his novels, he has here personified the mimosa flower as a human, using its blossoming and languishing life cycle as his theme.

9. "El hombre de los pies grandes" ("The Man with Big Feet"). Federico was born with such big feet that he learned to walk earlier and was steadier than most infants. This made him seem more settled and sedate than other children. He was always serious in school and seemed to learn by concentrating on his feet, a fact which he concealed from others. His first job was in a bank where he inspired confidence because of his stolid manner. He moved ahead rapidly in the business world, for he imparted a feeling of security to all, and everyone trusted him. When he was finally appointed national Minister of the Interior, the entire country rejoiced, viewing his appointment as a triumph of integrity. Inevitably, however, he one day, quite literally "put his foot in it." Having such a big foot, his error was naturally a major one: he ended his first year as Minister with a financial deficit of 1,672,483,561 *pesetas*.

D. La hiperestésica (The Hypersensitive Woman), *1931. (Collection)*

This slim volume contains only the four following stories.

1. "La hiperestésica" ("The Hypersensitive Woman"). The hypersensitive Elvira is left a large inheritance by her parents. After she dismisses most of the old servants because they irritate her for one reason or another, she begins to travel a great deal, always carrying her own bed linens, furniture and food, for she fears germs and bugs everywhere.

One day, she notices a jewel in the portrait of one of her ancestors and seeks it in her jewel box. Not finding it, she is convinced that she has been robbed and dedicates herself to the mission of finding it. At a party she sees the Marquesa de Nación wearing a three-leafed jewel like the one she is seeking and accuses her publicly of stealing it. When the noblewoman proves that she inherited the gem, Elvira, humiliated, apologizes and later tries to commit suicide. The doctor who saves her life falls in love with her and they marry. When she

Fiction: Novelettes

eventually has a baby girl she becomes more nervous than ever. One day, shrieking "No one will ever seduce her," she kills the new-born infant and subsequently herself dies of a hemorrhage.

In this exaggerated novelette, Ramón has carried the protagonist's excitable, high-strung condition to its logical extreme.

2. "El regalo del doctor" ("A Gift for the Doctor"). When the beautiful Celia Dufine and her husband, Rafael Pinto, arrive in Spain from Peru, they are such a stunning couple that they attract attention wherever they go. Even at the opera she stands out and, always, his good looks are the only suitable match for hers. When Rafael becomes ill, the doctor who attends him begins to visit the house daily and even twice daily, more to see Celia than his patient. Rafael, recuperating, becomes aware of the situation. Noticing his improvement, Celia, who has spent long weeks indoors, decides to go out and overdresses noticeably to do so. She visits the doctor's office several times, but surprises him by not being an easy conquest and merely chatting with him. Rafael, meanwhile, watches the situation carefully. When Celia finally consents to begin an affair with the doctor, she is repulsed when he attempts to make love to her on a chaise longue in his consulting room, and leaves upset. He then realizes that he really wants and loves her.

On the day the doctor releases him, Rafael has his accounts prepared and the fees for all visits calculated. He remarks, however, that since it is also customary to give the doctor a present, aware of their attraction for one another and of their clandestine relationship, he proffers him his wife, explaining that he will get a divorce. Although the doctor protests, Rafael is firmly insistent. Then, he calls Celia and informs her that he has paid the doctor and decided, moreover, to grant him the gift he knows he will most appreciate — her. Celia, exposed and defeated, at first protests, but later, with "that boldness of infidelity which is stupendous in women,"[7] leaves for a hotel. After she leaves, Rafael's composure disintegrates and the last paragraph states, "Only he had come undone in that conflict, and he allowed himself to fall into the armchair as when a curtain falls on the last act of a drama."[8]

The ending is an appropriate one, for this highly theatrical story reads like a play. Indeed, it seems curious that it was not written in drama form, for the dialogue here is realistic; the analysis and presentation of conflicting emotions is good. The final scene, in which the husband gets the upper hand and saves his dignity, is totally in keeping with Spanish attitudes. The theme of feminine fickleness and infidelity is frequent enough in Ramón to arouse conjecture about his personal experiences with women. Here it is handled in typically Spanish fashion as the unfaithful wife gets her deserved comeuppance.

3. "La roja" ("The Red-Head"). Upset because he believed his poetic muse had caused his daughter to be born a red-head, Celia's father feared that no one would want to marry her, so he had her trained to be a teacher. Although Celia developed into a shapely and pretty young lady, her family continued to view her redheadedness as a calamity, and in compensation granted her every whim and demand. After frightening away her first boyfriend by her extreme possessiveness, Celia began to traipse the streets looking for a man. She did meet a worthless youth but, following him home one day, she learned that he was married. After that, she began to make up fantastic stories about her romantic adventures: she had a child in Paris; she was seeing a widower with children, and so on. Determined to learn the truth, her distressed parents finally searched her room and discovered "love letters" to the widower. Confronted with this "evidence," Celia admitted that her amorous adventures existed only in her imagination. Shortly thereafter, realizing her need for love and consideration, her father obtained a teaching post for her in a small town, where he felt the townspeople would love and respect her; full of illusions, she went there.

This plot idea is too simple to be well sustained, even by Ramón in the twenty-two pages he devotes to it. Although the incongruity of red hair in Spain may have appealed to Gómez de la Serna as a subject, he failed to make it the calamitous accident of birth he apparently meant it to be.

4. "El vegetariano" ("The Vegetarian"). Don Hortensio, a zealous vegetarian, insists that his wife and daughter (ironically named Encarna and Purita, respectively) share his diet. Servants, obliged to do the same, refuse to stay, and his lifelong friend and neighbor, Pedro, obdurately resists his pressure to become a vegetarian. When Ramiro, Pedro's son, falls in love with Purita, he coaxes her to sample a ham sandwich which she eats in the privacy of her bedroom.

Timid and blushing at their next encounter, like an eager virgin newly initiated in carnal pleasure, she shyly asks him for another sample of the forbidden fruit and Ramiro furtively provides her

Fiction: Novelettes [77]

another sandwich. When her mother suffers from a headache, Purita convinces her to eat one and, so delicious do they both find the forbidden taste of meat, that they begin to purchase ham sandwiches surreptitiously, and eat them in the privacy of their swimming cabin on the beach. Apprised of the situation through an anonymous letter, Don Hortensio demands their promise to forego meat, but Ramiro asserts his rights as Purita's future spouse and carries her off to live with a responsible married couple until their wedding can take place. Permitted by her guardians to eat meat, Purita soon becomes rosy and healthier looking than she has ever been. Doña Encarna writes Hortensio that she plans a divorce, and moves in with Pedro's meat-eating family.

Enroute to Purita's wedding, she and her mother visit the obstinate Hortensio, begging him to attend. Impressed by their healthy appearance, he attends the wedding and, to the astonishment of all, eats meat at the banquet. He insists, nevertheless, that every child born of the marriage be raised a vegetarian, claiming that a child started on vegetables from birth (unlike his own impure generation) would be incorruptibly and healthily vegetarian.

This amusing tale about the circumventing of a vegetarian's obstinacy and scruples is narrated with humor and compassion for the foibles, weaknesses, and rationalizations of human nature.

E. El cólera azul (Blue Cholera), *1937. (Collection)*

The largest of Ramón's collections, this volume contains the following eleven short novels.

1. "El cólera azul" ("Blue Cholera"). Doña María de la Concepción and her mother, from Angola, vacationing in Lisbon, are inseparable. One day, however, because her mother has a headache, the younger woman goes out alone to make some necessary small purchases and, en route home, stops for refreshments in a tearoom. Upon leaving, she drops some packages which are retrieved by a courteous, monocled gentleman who then accompanies her to her hotel, and gallantly promises to await her in the lobby. Disconcertingly, however, the hotel proprietor and two gentlemen with black gloves meet her at the hotel entrance and accompany her to her room. Alarmed, she inquires for her mother and hurries to the door of her adjoining room, only to find that it is not only unoccupied, but even has different furniture, decor, and wallpaper than she

remembers! When she asks if it is room number 72, they tell her there is no such room number! When she asks the maid where her mother is, the maid answers that she was not accompanied by any "mother." Distressed, María insists upon seeing the hotel register, and finds her own name listed, but not her mother's. She realizes that the gentleman who accompanied her is no longer in the lobby and she feels that her last hope is gone. The two black-gloved gentlemen reappear and ask her to get into a car with them. She does but faints in the car and wakens the next day in a hospital. There, a nurse explains that her mother had suffered an attack of blue cholera and died while she was out. Because the disease was highly contagious, the hotel and the city wanted to conceal its existence. Hence, the plan she had encountered. She learned that she was in the Hospital de Medicina Tropical — as was the gentleman who had accompanied her, both isolated because of their exposure to the disease. After days and weeks pass, she asks if the gentleman may visit her. He gallantly does so, and falls in love with her. He proposes, she accepts, and they plan to marry when the forty-day quarantine is lifted.

The plot idea here is a novel and interesting one. A variation of this theme exists in a movie concerning a brother and sister in Paris in which a young woman loses her brother, his room, and so on.[9] The plot, with its elements of suspense, climax, and denouement, is well worked out, brief, and to the point with nothing superfluous.

2. "Peluquería feliz" ("The Cheerful Barbershop"). A young man continues to patronize the barbershop of his childhood because of its cheerful atmosphere. Familiar with the clients and barbers there for years, he feels he can even read their thoughts. Often the pretty daughter or the wife of the owner passes through the shop as she enters or leaves their adjacent apartment. Eventually, a swarthy client who comes to be shaved twice daily attracts the youth's attention, for something about him portends evil. Then, ominously, Don Ernesto, the shopkeeper, begins to sell black canaries to satisfy the numerous patrons who have offered to buy his songbird. Vaguely uncomfortable, the narrator omits his usual visits to the barbershop for a period. When he returns to his "happy shop," he finds everything in darkness and the collected neighbors commenting on that afternoon's tragedy. They tell him that Don Ernesto had used his barber's razor to cleanly slit the throats of his daughter and the swarthy client when he caught them making love in his apartment at the rear of the shop. Then, after killing his wife for permitting their relations, he

Fiction: Novelettes [79]

had killed himself. Disconsolate, the narrator wanders the streets wondering where to go henceforth for his haircuts and finally decides to stay at home and have a barber come in. He feels sad and depressed, as if he has now lost part of his childhood forever.

3. "La estufa de cristal" ("The Greenhouse"). This is a dreamlike fantasy story in which the narrator frequents a rose garden while "she" (his beloved) is ill and dying. One night, upon entering the greenhouse, he encounters a mysterious woman who almost seduces him, although she warns him that surrender means death. When a rose he is looking at suddenly loses all its petals, it seems to him an omen that "she" is past the crisis and he flees. "She" recovers. When together they visit the rose garden some time later, he relates the incident to her and she realizes that her fever broke while he was there, for at that same time she had dreamed that she was in a greenhouse and that her fever dropped away like rose petals.

4. "La niña Alcira" ("The Young Alcira"). Luis Pesoea, a young man of about twenty, from Lisbon, goes to Río de Janeiro to visit relatives and to investigate career possibilities. At the beach, he meets the lovely fourteen-year-old Alcira Nantes. He continues seeing the girl until her father, who is about thirty-five, visits him to complain that he and his twenty-nine-year-old wife are distressed that Alcira, so young, is in love. They do not want her to repeat their story of a too early marriage. He warns Luis to stay away from the young girl.

Luis seeks solace in a Negress cigar vendor and takes her to the beach. There at dusk as he passionately embraces her, he hears Alcira weeping as her father, attempting to shock the girl out of her infatuation, confronts her with the situation. Shortly thereafter, the Negress stops seeing Luis and he finds himself alone. Occasionally he encounters some of Alcira's friends, but they seem to laugh at him. One day the newspaper carries the shocking story that Alcira Nantes has burned herself alive. Distressed, he visits Delia, a friend of Alcira's, to find out what happened, and she reproaches him for the incident with the Negress, telling him that it precipitated Alcira's suicide. Luis feels he can no longer stay in Río de Janeiro. He tells his relatives about Alcira and her tragic end and arranges to leave the city.

In this story the dialogues between Luis and Alcira often seem like series of *greguerías,* rich in ornate and fanciful metaphors. While it is unlikely that young lovers would speak on such a high literary plane, the richness of metaphor lends the tale a legend-like, poetic aura.

   5. "El defensor del cementerio" ("The Defender of the Cemetery"). When a group of speculators plan to demolish the local cemetery and clear the site for building, Don Amadeo Paloma, an old bachelor who visits his father's grave daily, leads the town's concerned citizens in fight against that action. During the ensuing series of judicial appeals, the neglected cemetery becomes a target for thieves who steal zinc roofing and frames from the corridors of niches, causing them to cave in. Many of the dead have to be removed, transferred elsewhere, and reburied. Both the living and the dead are distressed, and engage in numerous dialogues expressing their concern and anxiety. Workmen entering the cemetery to begin clearing it are shot at by a sniper, and police and civil guards are called to rout out the "armed protestors." When they finally close in and kill the sniper, they find that it is Don Amadeo who, holed up in a mausoleum, has held them off with his life.

   6. "Suspensión del destino" ("Postponement of Destiny"). On a cloudy and threatening day, everyone is uncertain whether or not the bullfight will be canceled. If it is called off before starting, the people's money is refunded and the bulls are saved. Everywhere bets are made on the outcome. The bullfight starts and the first bull, Azafrán, destined for the toreador, Páramo, comes out. The rain starts and turns into a real downpour. The fight is called off, and, since it turns out that Azafrán was destined to kill his next toreador, Páramo's death is postponed. Páramo himself feels a great sense of relief at the postponement. After seeing the bull he had had a strange foreboding, followed by an enormous sigh of relief. At the next scheduled fight, Azafrán kills the toreador. The story's last sentence reiterates that "the showers had been a gift of fortune" for Páramo.

   7. "Los destrozonas" ("The Roughnecks"). Remigio sets out for the carnival, dressed as a roughneck, and pairs up with an unknown man similarly disguised. Emboldened by their disguises, they swagger through the streets with an ever growing desire to cause trouble. On the outskirts of town, they are surrounded by a threatening group of about twenty masked figures and, to divert them away from himself, Remigio suggests that they all visit the nearby house of "Mary, the cancerous woman." The bedridden woman and her

sister, taken aback by the boisterous invaders, offer them wine. The revelers sing and dance in her sickroom until, unexpectedly, the floor and the house cave in and all are tumbled to the ground under masses of debris. When help comes, the injured and dead revelers, grotesque in their costumes, are removed from the rubble, presenting a picture not soon to be forgotten by future carnivalgoers.

8. "Las consignatarias" ("Women of Assignation"). Ramón ardently desires Gracia, a beautiful flirt. Of all the men she has had (mostly ship captains whose ships have docked in Málaga), only one, the captain of the "Estuardo" really mattered to her. When Ramón's perseverance is finally rewarded with an assignation, he arranges to meet her in the quietest, most secluded place he can think of — the English cemetery. She arrives, and, as they seek a sheltered place in which to make love, she reads tombstones along the way. Unexpectedly, she encounters a tombstone dedicated to the captain of the "Estuardo" and, weeping, translates it for Ramón. Realizing that her sad find has caused him to forever lose his opportunity with her, he resolves thereafter never to have another assignation in a cemetery.

9. "Se presentó el hígado" ("His Liver Presented Itself"). Rodolfo, over twenty now and rapidly gaining weight, one day receives a caller who introduces himself as his liver — explaining that one's liver usually presents itself at about this period of life. Thereafter, Rodolfo is constantly aware of the intruder's presence. They converse and even argue frequently, until eventually his liver makes itself felt even in the secret hours he shares with his pretty young mistress. To meet as many fellow sufferers as possible, he arranges a Liverian Congress where, impressed by one sufferer's recommendation to quiet a complaining liver by drinking gin, he assiduously does so thereafter.

Liver ailments are a common complaint of Europeans, and the Spanish expression for becoming aware of a disorder is to say *se presentó*, ("it presented itself"). In this story, Ramón has based his theme upon a deliberately misleading but literal interpretation of that concept.

10. "Ella + Ella - El + El" ("She + She - He + He"). Despite the fact that the well-to-do Ibizas, Soledad and Fermín, entertain a great deal, Eduardo is their only intimate friend. Although this

childless couple has a more harmonious relationship than any married couple he knows, he cannot help feeling that some mysterious secret, shared by the maid, hangs over their household. To his own surprise, he finds himself physically attracted to Soledad, who had been a friend of his mother's, and senses a response on her part. Then, noticeable discord begins to mar the harmony of the Ibiza household and relationship. Finally, one evening, a totally distraught Soledad confesses to him the secret she had vowed to carry to the grave: Fermín is a woman. When he promises to guard her secret, Soledad hysterically insists that it must be revealed, and thereupon makes the same startling announcement to her other assembled guests, who greet it with mixed reactions.

The theme of homosexual or lesbian love is not unusual in Ramón. Here, as elsewhere, it seems to be the element of the exotic and the mysterious that he is exploiting, rather than the erotic or sexual.

11. "Pueblo de morenas" ("The Town of the Brunettes"). The town of Alburquerque on the Andalusian coast is chosen by the Englishman, Mr. Sender, as the beach from which to send out underwater ocean cables to England. A crew of blond Englishmen coming to tend the cables is immediately impressed by the dark beauty of Alburquerque's women. The Englishmen think they are conquering the dark Spanish beauties, but actually it is they who are falling in love.

The neglected cable becomes restless and breaks; messages are garbled, and Sender warns his crew that all fraternizers will be fired. The love affairs become secret, but continue. Distressed English mothers send warning letters to their sons. Alburquerque's only blonde is besieged by suitors who can court her without incurring the reprisals attached to courting the forbidden brunettes. A rescue mission, composed of the Englishmen's sisters, is sent to Alburquerque, but the rescuers all form friendships with the dark Spanish beauties, and are abruptly returned to England. After one illegal emergency marriage takes place and the couple leaves for America, the remaining Englishmen are immediately dispersed to different posts, and Alburquerque has a moment of peace.

When a second group of Englishmen arrives, however, the same thing happens. News of the situation brings tourists to Alburquerque. The city grows, chalets and hotels spring up. The mayor and the city council attempt to solve the problem by ruling that all brunettes must dye their hair blond. When they do, the Englishmen

Fiction: Novelettes

are even more attracted by the striking combination of dark eyes and blond hair. When two more girls marry English crewmen, the English complain and the town Council rescinds the order.

Smirl, a young English nobleman, traveling incognito, disappears in Alburquerque. Eventually cable service deteriorates completely as the English neglect it to spend more time with their sweethearts, and finally, England sends Spain a note requesting the dissolution of the city and the removal of the cable to a different location. Concerned, the Spanish government decrees the removal of the *morenas* to other cities in equal distribution, and the removal of the cable to an uninhabited region. England sends Spain a message of gratitude.

II *Superhistorical Novels*

A. Doña Juana la loca (Doña Juana the Mad), *1944. (Collection)*

In a vein similar to that used twenty-two years earlier in his pseudoregional novels, Ramón wrote another group of tales based on history or legend which he half humorously called "superhistorical" novels. They are really novelettes. Their composition, he tells us in the prologue,[10] blends together both the historic and hypothetical past. Since history never happened as was supposed or as documents relate it, the "superhistorian's" task is to collect its divagations and to present its futuristic, supersubconscious and superidealistic interpretations rather than its usual materialistic and vulgar ones.

1. "Doña Juana la loca" ("Doña Juana The Mad"). Ramón's version of Doña Juana's true story presents the hapless queen as obsessed both by the fear of death and by an inordinately possessive love of her husband, Philip the Fair. In this "superhistoric" version, Philip dies of a fever contracted when he casually drinks a glass of contaminated water after a ball game with his courtiers. The queen encases his embalmed corpse in armor to shield him from the amorous glances she suspects even from abbesses in whose convents she seeks hospitality during her endless pilgrimage through the realm, and circulates the legend (more in keeping with his dignity and her madness) that he was bitten by the lion representing Leon, painted on his throne. When her son assumes power, he orders his mother confined to a church tower, and the king's coffin placed in the nave of the church below, where, from a small window she may keep watch over it. The bereaved queen one day throws herself from the window to be united with him. Ramón's "superhistorical" story

stresses the madness, the faith in magic and charlatans, and the hallucinatory imaginings which traditionally characterized the mad queen. The unhistoric suicide of the finale improves upon history by providing a more dramatic conclusion to her story.

2. "Doña Urraca de Castilla" ("Doña Urraca of Castile"). This story is based entirely upon the fantasy that Doña Urraca (whose name means "magpie") was truly a magpie. In the prologue to this work, Ramón writes, "It occurred to me that she did represent those black and white birds with wide wings and long tails that fly overhead on those hot Castilian days . . . that she felt herself one of them."[11] He imagines the queen transforming herself into a bird by night and flying out from her bedroom window. Going a step further, he imagines her at rest in a tree, recognizing her close friend and confidant, the constable Yllán in a similar bird. Thereafter, the two birds meet often, sharing a nocturnal royal secret. One night, however, a royal fletcher sees a magpie flying over the grape arbor attracted by its fondness for grapes; the fletcher looses an arrow, mortally wounding the bird-queen. Urraca struggles back to her room where she explains that she accidentally intercepted the arrow when leaning over her balcony to investigate noises below. She dies, and Yllán, her bird-friend, is never seen again.

3. "El caballero de Olmedo" ("The Gentleman from Olmedo") is Ramón's whimsical variation of the legend popularized by Lope de Vega under the same title. Ramón presents the popular hero as Damián García, a handsome youth who lives with his widowed mother and whose presence enhances every gathering it graces. Damián's disdainful refusals of overtures of marriage from wealthy women aroused comments in Olmedo. Even Soledad, the loveliest daughter of Olmedo, found her interest in him unrewarded and turned her glances toward Deogracias, Olmedo's second most comely youth. Often Damián, who lived next door to a seminary, wondered if his vocation might not be to become a priest, a cardinal, or a pope, for he felt, somehow, that he was destined for greatness. One day, his mother confided to him the secret that he was not her husband's son, but a royal bastard, the son of King Henry. The king, despite three wives, had died heirless precisely when he was en route to Medina to meet his only son, and perhaps to recognize him legally. No written proof or record of this royal paternity exists, however, and the king's untimely death left them with only the lifelong pensions he had earlier assigned them. After Damián learns this, his air of

Fiction: Novelettes   [85]

mystery and tragedy deepens. Deogracias becomes increasingly attracted to him and the two become inseparable companions. This angers Soledad and arouses the hatred of Amado, Deogracias' formerly inseparable squire, who plots revenge. One night, en route home, Damián stops in a sweetshop for a snack and upon leaving is attacked in the dark street outside. A dagger is thrust into his back and the story concludes with the traditional refrain from the popular folk song, which is the basis of the legend: " 'Twas at night they killed/The Caballero,/The Jewel of Medina,/The Flower of Olmedo."

Ramón's tampering with the legend and his wry inference of homosexuality have the effect of humor because of the unexpectedness of the plot twists for those who are familiar with the traditional story. The *caballero's* illegitimate royal origin adds stature to his figure, and deepens the aura of tragedy and mystery in the work.

4. "La emparedada de Burgos" ("The Recluse of Burgos"). Burgos had its most famous recluse in Doña Ana of Austria, who voluntarily retired to the Monastery of Silos. There, in the isolation of her walled-off cell, she had only one opening through which food was passed, and through which she occasionally spoke with a rare visitor. She spent her time in prayer, meditation, and preparation for death. When her husband returned from the Crusades, learned of his wife's enclosure, and found that his only child, a daughter, had entered a cloistered convent, he removed the girl on pretext of illness and appealed to the king to effect his wife's release. The king, fearful that such a royal order might upset relations with Austria, turned to Rome for a decision. The Church ruled ambiguously that because of the prince's service in the Crusades, it would *not oppose* her release. Realizing that embarrassment at returning to Burgos, where she had taken leave of her friends for life, was the basis for his wife's reluctance to leave her enclosure, the prince took her instead to Verdin where *encamadas* (penitential promises to stay abed, in a sort of semiretirement) were in vogue. There, all three (they and their daughter) retired to their perpetual beds.

Once ensconced, they heard the town crier proclaiming war with Austria, and realized that their unorthodox marital sharing of a supposedly penitential bed had upset the delicate balance of history.

This is a delightfully told story, replete with amusing details and climaxed with a humorously unexpected ending. It evinces once again how the transforming powers of Ramón's wit and humor work upon even the most unlikely themes.

5. "La Beltraneja" ("Beltran's Daughter"). Ramón presents the blonde Queen Isabel as plotting to rid herself of claims made to the Spanish throne by her brother's only child, who is so commonly believed to be illegitimate that she is openly called "Beltran's Daughter" after the royal favorite believed to be her father. Isabel arranges an uprising in the very household of the dark Beltraneja, planting Captain Gofrán among the Beltraneja's men to win her confidence. His task is to carry her off to "shelter" when the uprising occurs, to a palace Isabel has provided him in Granada. Unexpectedly, Gofrán's reward is double, for as Ramón's manipulation of history would have it, not only is he rewarded by Isabel, but he also falls in love with the Beltraneja.

6. "Los adelantados" ("The Explorers"). In this story, Ramón presents seven gentlemen, all dreamers, who, interested not in glory, wealth or conquests, but merely in the pure joy of discovering a new world, leave Pizarro's company and strike out on their own, on a peaceful venture of discovery. Pure adventurers, they are ecstatic with the newness of all they see. The forest, trees, and animals all sense that they are explorers rather than exploiters and help them. When they fall among hostile Indians, they use a mirror to reflect the sunlight, temporarily blinding the chief. Awed by their power, he fetes them, and during the celebration they steal away. When they arrive at the city of the Incas, they are well treated, shown the temples of the sun and of the moon and the convent of the virgins, and sped along their way. They leave, sniffing the air about them "as if they were smelling the last shores of perfect serenity."[12]

7. "Los siete infantes de Lara" ("The Seven Princes of Lara"). Ramón bases his version of this tale on the premise that the legendary strength of the seven princes comes precisely from their being seven. One day, when hunting, they catch a gazelle, who is really a nymph, and decide to watch over her through the night and return her to the woods next day, mindful of a warning which Juan, the oldest, had received from a gypsy, that misfortune would befall them from hunting. Don Juan and Don Manuel stand guard over her through the night, and fall so deeply in love that by morning, when she escapes, they have become fused into one person — Don Juan

Manuel. The group tries to conceal this by never appearing simultaneously, but eventually some suspicions are aroused. The King of Castile sends an artist to paint their portrait, as a ruse to uncover the truth. Don Juan Manuel tries to deceive him by exiting and reentering wearing different clothes. The artist pretends to be taken in, but informs the king. The king has them killed and publishes the fact that the seven princes are dead, explaining that history required no explanations — if the legend mentioned seven, the number should be kept intact.

All seven of Ramón's "superhistorical" novels are, in reality, novelettes or short stories, for none exceeds twenty-five pages. All have well-conceived and well-executed plots, and are, essentially, clever distortions of historical or legendary tales. Ramón's tendency to play with reality, blending it with fantasy, was as irresistible in the realm of the historical and traditional as in the realms of fiction or biography. Reality, for him, had no barriers. His imagination colored whatever he perceived, transforming it into a more poetic and colorful "reality" of his own creation.

III *Novelettes*

Five of the short novels Ramón published independently were not included in any subsequent volume of collected novelettes. These five, treated below, differ greatly from one another, but all are engaging short novels and the reason for their omission from the collections is not apparent.

A. "Leopoldo y Teresa" ("Leopold and Teresa"), 1922. Leopold, a typically bohemian ramonesque hero, lives on a small inheritance left him by his aunt, and spends his days sitting on park benches, seeking the "right" woman to share his life and sink uncomplainingly into degradation with him when his money gives out. One day, he meets Teresa, an attractive, sad, and innocent-looking young woman. When he learns that she is a naïve orphan living unhappily with an aunt, he seduces her.

After intercourse she asks naïvely if he will now marry her and, touched by her innocence and her trust, he says that he will. They buy used furniture and set up an apartment. He also buys her a dress, and is pleased with the way it sets off the graceful young figure she is innocently unaware of. Since she never refuses him anything and always does exactly as he says, he is completely content, and they spend long leisurely afternoons simply walking, sitting on park benches, or looking in store windows. She turns ever prettier and Leopoldo is happy when she becomes pregnant, believing that this will tie her firmly to him. He resolves that their son will grow up in the same poor but happy manner, enjoying the free and pleasant public gardens of Madrid.

Perhaps this novelette should have been titled simply, "A Man and a Woman," for the essence of this plot lies in its basically unadorned simplicity. It is a story about a simple man fortunate in finding an equally simple woman. Two free and uncomplicated spirits, they meet, marry, and beget a child. This is life reduced to its lowest common human denominators, a ramonesque state of innocence without the complications and frustrations of careers, ambitions, and unfulfilled desires.

B. "La abandonada en el Rastro" ("The Woman Abandoned in the Flea Market"), 1929, is a novelette which utilizes incidents and descriptions taken from Ramón's earlier work, *The Flea Market*. It is a story about a Spaniard who misses his train at a station in France, sees in this the hand of destiny, and consequently marries Renée, a French girl fascinated by all things Spanish. After they return to Spain, they frequently visit the Flea Market — a development which provides Ramón with a new motive for detailed descriptions of the Market. Bored with Renée's continuous search for old things in the Market, the protagonist one day locks her in the back room of an antique shop where she is rummaging about, and goes off. Left alone, she disintegrates into her component parts: hair, dental plate, corset, glass eye — all the incongruous things that make up the Market. In a way, the market has been personified in her.

C. "El hijo surrealista" ("The Surrealist Son"), 1930, is the story of Henri Kloz, the rebellious son of a typical bourgeois family, who devotes himself to frenetically "subverting" existence. He fathers the child of the caretaker's daughter, has epic arguments with his father (indicative of the "generation gap" between them), destroys the faces on numerous masterpieces in the art museum with sulphuric acid, deliberately breaks the knicknacks in a department store window, and is arrested for writing threatening letters to the nation's president. He is eventually ejected by his father who, understandably fed up with his excesses, refuses to accept the explanation that his actions are those of a misunderstood "surrealist." Again, Ramón has based a story on a whimsical semantic interpretation. If a surrealist is, literally, one who is "above reality," he cannot be expected to conform to the "realistic" standards and mores of others.

D. "Aventuras y desgracias de un sinsombrerista" ("The Trials and Adventures of a Non-hatter"), 1932. In this whimsical, semibiographical tale, Ramón tells of an angelic visitation which announced to him the advantages of *sinsombrerismo* (hatlessness). Thereafter, defying convention, he went about with his head bared to the heavens, seeing much more than he had before. Reproved for his unconventional hatlessness, he always defended his position. *Sinsombrerismo* became his characteristic, and soon other young men, picking up the idea, decided to hold a convention of radical *sinsombreristas*. When traditionalists pursued him with offers of free hats, he feared that he might be assassinated by one of them, and become a martyr of the hatless movement. On a trip to Buenos Aires, however, he fell in love with a lovely Jewish orphan named Sarah, who informed him that since all Jewish men wore hats even at home, he would have to wear one if he married her. Flight seemed to be their only recourse and, to escape unrecognized, he disguised himself completely by simply wearing a hat! This is a whimsical fun story, suggested perhaps by the notoriously hatless Ramón's meeting with his Jewish wife Luisa's family in Buenos Aires.

E. "El turco de los nardos" ("The Turk With the Spikenards"), 1943. This novelette is set in a predominantly foreign section on the outskirts of a large city where Poles, Italians, Lithuanians, and a large number of Turks have congregated. The outstanding Turkish family is that of Muley Yrak whose daughter Xenia is the suburb's loveliest maiden. Jorge, a Spanish youth, is secretly in love with Xenia, as is Christian Bander, son of the principal Lithuanian family. When Christian adds a second story to the Yrak home, and buys furniture, it becomes plain that he plans to marry Xenia and move into the second floor. Jorge, feigning indifference, keeps company with the Polish Nelia.

Conscious of the envious resentment surrounding them, the Yraks give a Christmas party for their neighbors at which everyone gets drunk. The Poles and Lithuanians, following their custom at festivals, break their glasses. Jorge, after arguing with Christian, declares himself publicly to Xenia, who accepts him, stating that they will repay Christian for building the second floor. Jorge's father refuses to lend him the money for this, and in explanation reveals his secret. As a young man, he exhumed a corpse and burned it in his carriage with his own identification, in order to collect his life insurance. With the money, he and his wife fled to America. Such hard-won money, he explains, must not be spent foolishly. Moreover, Jorge must not do anything that might attract the attention of the law.

Unfortunately, however, Jorge had once given his father's Spanish passport to Nelia so that she could see his baby picture, and had allowed her to keep it. When the Poles and Lithuanians meet to plan their revenge, Christian's mother suggests sending the passport to Spain for investigation. When this is done, the fingerprints are traced and the crime discovered. Soon after, the police arrest Jorge's father for the "murder" of the victim found in his carriage.

This story of brooding revenge is set poetically in an ambient heavy with the sweet fragrance of the spikenards in the Turk's garden, which seems to influence the passions of all involved. Its well-constructed plot and sparse dialogue effectively build up to a dramatic climax. Following Ramón's practice, this novel skillfully emphasizes mood, feeling, and ambient. The denouement is rapid, decisive, complete.

IV *Short Stories*

In addition to his "short novels," which most critics would consider short stories, Ramón also wrote a number of compositions which he termed *cuentos* or stories. They are frequently (but not necessarily) shorter than his novelettes. The first of these appear as appendices to a rather curious work which has not heretofore been discussed, called *Morbideces (Morbidities),* and are, on the whole, exaggerated and somewhat adolescent stories, rightly ignored by most critics. Sixteen years later, Ramón published a collection of stories for children which, although charming in its simplicity, is important only in that it is indicative of his creative desire to essay every literary channel. *Cuentos de fin de año* (Year-end Tales), written by a middle-aged Ramón, reveals the still youthful literary attitude of their writer as he attempted somewhat elementary experiments with juxtapositions of spatial and temporal planes in stories projecting into future and past times. They also reveal the pathos which came to characterize the aging humorist, for many of the stories simply crystallize nostalgic reminiscences of bygone times. Although another collection, *Cuentos para los días de no salir de casa (Stories for Stay-at-Home Days),* appears on all recent biographical listings of Gómez de la Serna's works, the present author has been unable to locate and review the work.

A. *Morbideces (Morbidities), 1908.* This is a curious book, betraying in almost every line the intellectual pretensions and immaturity of its twenty-year-old author. Its 122 pages of "abstract" autobiography comprise a kind of diary of Ramón's intimate ideas and beliefs at that time, rather than a factual account of his life, although in the prologue, he pretends that the work is a manuscript he received in confidence from a young friend who did not want it published. For no clear reason other than, perhaps, their morbidity, five very short stories ranging in length from two to nine pages are appended. The long essay section of the work alternately serves as an outlet for the young writer's unfulfilled sensual desires, or a "position paper" on his hygienic, gastronomic, historical, emotional, literary, aesthetic, moral, and other values. He tells us, for example, that he deliberately flees crystallized ideas, judgments, or opinions to seek a virginal vision and spirit; he exalts his individuality and negates common values; he perceives voluptuousness and egoism as the leitmotiv of human acts, and considers great men and heroes essentially egoists of exorbitant discipline. Our ethical system, he asserts, is traditionally and erroneously imposed upon us.

Even at this early age, Ramón's deep feeling for Madrid is evident as he describes his impressions of its museums, educational institutions, streets, bars, plazas, and so on. In his youthful arrogance, Ramón makes derogatory evaluations of the writers of the Generation of '98, and even reflects tolerantly upon his own former youthful dilettantism and enthusiasm. He expresses a vague belief in the heart, the soul, love, and altruism, and waxes almost poetically sentimental when he describes his ideal "Corregioseraphic" type woman. *Morbidities* is basically an exercise in writing by a young man attempting to find himself, as he expresses his innermost, incoherent emotions and thoughts, and seeks to understand and evaluate them. In concluding, the young writer affects a majestic indifference toward existence, describing the endless, pointless routine of the ordinary events in his life, attendance at the Ateneo, at University classes, and other activities. At the conclusion of his "thought diary," Ramón comments that he will append a few short stories written when he felt that he "still had feelings."

1. "El ciego y la hetaira" ("The Blind Man and the Courtesan"). The first story tells of a courtesan who compassionately cleansed the wounded forehead of a blind mendicant. When a passerby remarked upon the appearance and nature of his Samaritan, the blind man's expression of innocent gratitude turned to one of greedy lust.

Frustrated and angry, the woman slapped him and walked away, her one moment of disinterested compassion denied her.

2. "El apestado" ("The Diseased One"). The narrator of this story receives a letter from a rural relative, informing him that he has lost his vision and is now in Madrid. Upon visiting him, he is horrified to find him not only blind, but also covered with ulcerous, foul-smelling sores. The sick man tells him a story of a casual encounter with an apparently innocent young girl, and the subsequent manifestations of his disease. He tells how he later returned to his wife, thinking himself cured, only to learn, after begetting an idiot son, that his illness had merely been in a quiescent state. The "diseased one," dying now, bids farewell to the narrator.

The exaggerated picture of a grotesquely disease-ridden syphilitic betrays the very youthful imagination of its young author.

3. "La doncella" ("The Serving Maid"). This simple tale about the daydreams of an innocent and pretty young serving maid concerning the admiration men will someday show her, stresses their sad contrast with the poor reality of her life. There is an almost autobiographic element to the contrast of aspirations and reality Ramón depicts here.

4. "La muerte del lunático" ("The Death of a Lunatic"). A preliminary paragraph explains that this story was written when Ramón was inebriated. The two-page story concerns a poet, enamored of the moon, who makes a date with her for nighttime, in the garden. After a long wait, she comes. He sees her, naked, in the pool and throws himself into its depths, seeking her, thereby attaining the fittingly poetic death of a true lunatic. The theme is similar to that of Bécquer's "Los ojos verdes" ("The Green Eyes"). In its brevity, however, it seems more an exercise in the use of fantasy than a poetic evocation of mood and mystery.

5. "La caja de Pandora" ("Pandora's Box"). This is the final story of the group. Similar to the story of the serving maid, it describes the daydreams of a mother and her young daughter in cheap upper-gallery seats at the opera. Both dream of a brilliant future for the young girl. The mother sees her daughter as the great singer she had always longed to be, and the girl sees herself in the role of the heroine.

The blind man, the serving maid, the lunatic, and the operagoer — all have in common their unfulfilled aspirations and yearnings.

Fiction: Novelettes [93]

Only the diseased protagonist fulfilled his desires, and for this he paid a terrible price. Clearly, Ramón made every effort to have these brief stories live up to the general macabre title under which they appeared. They are, indeed, morbidities.

B. Cuentos para niños (Children's Tales), 1924

1. "Por los tejados" ("Along the Rooftops") is a fairy tale-like story about a child who, climbing to the rooftops to rescue his ball, has a series of exciting adventures as he goes "along the rooftops," including visits to the attics of good and bad witches, and the rescue of a three-year-old girl hidden away by an evil man.

2. "El marquesito en el circo" ("The Little Marquis at the Circus") tells of a little marquis who takes the place of a child clown in a circus number. An unexpected incident causes him to show great heroism, to the delight of his audience and the little girl who accompanies him.

3. "El bazar más suntuoso del mundo" ("The Biggest Bazaar in the World") blends fantasy and reality in the story of a child and his nursemaid wandering through a great toy bazaar, marveling at the toys and frightened by the toy animals. When the bazaar closes, the child remains behind, talking with the dolls who think he is a living doll.

So ingenuous are these tales in their simplicity that it seems they could have been written by a child. Ramón's essential childlikeness has been a true asset to him here.

C. Cuentos de fin de año (Year-end Tales)

This is a collection (published in 1947) of Christmas and year-end stories in which, as Ramón admits in the prologue, he seeks both the novel and nostalgic because he believes that at Christmas-time the old and the new converge.[13] The following stories are included in this collection.

1. "Olvido." In response to Ramón's desire to relive a past Christmas, a mysterious voice tells him that he may exchange three future Christmases for whichever one he chooses to relive. After studying the Christmas pictures in his old photo album, he makes his choice. The lights change and he finds himself under an old chandelier of bygone times. His parents are youthful, his brothers and sisters are children, yet, he himself remains mature. He falls in love with Olvido, a lovely young woman seated next to him at dinner.

After his return to the present, he inquires about her among his relatives, but, although she appears in the group picture for that Christmas, no one remembers her. Despite his realization that if she were adult that Christmas night, she would now be an old woman, Ramón cannot forget her.

2. "Nochebuena del año dos mil quinientos" ("Christmas Eve, 2500 A.D."). Given a choice by the Christmas angel of experiencing a past or future Christmas, Ramón chooses to experience Christmas 2500 A.D. Soon the room spins about him, and he finds himself in a space filled with strange light. A recorded voice instructs him to enter the dining room. Young people already assembled there seem to recognize him as an old "uncle." Although they wonder why he is dressed in "old-fashioned" clothes, they nevertheless enjoy the humor of it. Their synthetic skin and tight clothes are quite different from his; the room is illuminated by a sort of phosphorescent wall, and a moving sofa carries them about. In one of the youths present, he recognizes his father's voice and face, and suddenly he feels distressed and lost, anxious to return to the present, and aware that "playing with time was sheer madness."[14] He seeks the door to the hall as the room begins again to spin around him. When it stops, he finds himself once more at the desk in his office.

3. "Cena de académicos" ("Academicians' Supper"). When a group of aged professors gather at year's end to have toasts and drink, they cannot help wondering whose chair will be empty next year.

4. "La botella y el candelabro" ("The Bottle and the Candlestick"). This short story is in two parts. In the first, a poor couple happily celebrates a simple Christmas alone. The only gift the husband can afford for his wife is a candle which, having no adequate holder, they place in a bottle. This simple gift makes them inexpressibly happy and the night, unforgettable. Part Two takes place several years later. The couple has prospered and now, with a full candelabra, wonders how one lone candle could ever have pleased them. The candles flicker out until only one remains. They like it better, and realize that this is so because one candle, like love, unites two lives in one flame.[15]

5. "La tía Marta" ("Aunt Martha"). Aunt Martha arrives late and quarrelsome for the family Christmas dinner. Then, piqued at

not being seated at the table near the host, she leaves abruptly. Her actions spoil the holiday for the others, and the youthful narrator is sent to persuade her to return. When he arrives at her house, he finds her enjoying a candlelight dinner with a gentleman friend. Disillusioned, he returns home, commenting merely that she is all right. When his father teases him about his apparent distress at the absence of his "adored aunt," he leaves the room sobbing.

This simple story of adolescent disillusionment is especially poignant because of its holiday setting. The perceptiveness revealed here about an adolescent's sensitive feelings, although unusual in Ramón, is well handled, and no unwarranted humor mars his sympathetic treatment of the theme.

6. "El gabán de nieve" ("The Snow Coat"). Clotilde capriciously asks her playmates to make her a coat of snow. They cover her with snow to make a coat and collar which she says looks like mink. When they encircle her with a mocking singsong chant, she breaks out of the circle and runs home. There, her mother tells her to shake the snow from her coat, but she delays obeying, sensing a miraculous change in the coat. Irritated, her mother attempts to take the coat from her but, upon touching it, realizes by its softness that it is really mink! The fairy tale-like quality of this charmingly simple story makes it seem like a child's tale.

7. "El pandero de Rosaura" ("Rosaura's Tambourine"). Dana plays Rosaura's tambourine with such frenzy that a dark green Asturian bear appears in the doorway. When he softens the sound, the bear leaves. Onlookers who witnessed the scene are left unsure whether they saw or imagined it.

8. "El natalicio del poeta" ("The Birth of a Poet"). All the usual holiday sounds prevail in a poor tenement house until 2:00 A.M., when the sound of a woman's weeping silences them. When her cries end in the birth of a son, her neighbors comment that no one but a poet should dare be born on Christmas night; and the young man, in fact, turns out to be one.

9. "El creador de los nacimientos" ("The Christmas-Crib Maker"). Although Uncle Hannibal did little else all year but doze in an easy chair, just before Christmas he always busied himself mysteriously behind the locked door of the spare room, preparing his annual masterpiece. On Christmas Eve, opening the door with a

flourish, he would proudly present a nativity scene adorned with changing lights, running water, and other embellishments.

When his wife died and he remarried, he hesitated to visit the first wife's family again because of his sister-in-law's disapproval. Formerly related to the family by marriage, he felt that his new marriage had severed this tie. Although the family yearns to call and tell him that they miss him and his Christmas-crib scenes, no one does so, and they lose a veritable poet of Christmas-cribs.

10. "Cuento de Navidad con vidriera de colores" ("A Christmas Story About a Stained Glass Window"). Don Santiago had a stained glass window in his study. One night, when he inexplicably felt impelled to speak to them, the figures in it broke out and sat in the armchair beside him to chat. Irritated when they accused him of living in selfish isolation, he broke their glass forms with fireplace tongs. Early the following morning, he was found dead in his study and his death was attributed to double pneumonia brought on by wind and cold from the open window.

11. "El hidalgo y el maquinista" ("The Gentleman and the Machinist"). A poor gentleman, invited to Christmas supper by his neighbor, a sympathetic and kindly train conductor's wife, is surprised to see the accumulation of delicacies the conductor has picked up along the routes· of his different trips. The conductor comes in late, quite soiled. After he has washed up and joined the family, bringing yet more goodies, the man invited to dinner toasts him as "the gentleman of the future."[16]

12. "Fuera de casa" ("Dining Out"). Humoring his wife's desire not to eat Christmas dinner at home, a husband agrees to dine out. They walk a long time until they find a restaurant that suits them. The following Christmas, they do the same thing, ending up in a hotel restaurant, where they feel like "twentieth class" coach travelers. She then suggests that they eat at home the next year, saying she now realizes that Christmas is a day on which one should not feel lost, but at home.

13. "El viejo de las barbas de algodón" ("The White-Bearded Old Man"). In Paris, just as a simple family is about to sit down to Christmas dinner, a white-bearded man enters their apartment with some packages and two bottles of champagne, explaining that his

Fiction: Novelettes

key accidentally fits their lock. They invite him to join them for Christmas dinner and he accepts. During dinner they all enjoy him, but wonder why he looks a little familiar. Then, when he is ready to leave, he puts on a red cap and they all recognize him as Papa Noel! He smiles, thanks them for the dinner, and assures them that he has not been equally welcomed by the rich or the poor, but only by the middle class.

14. "Falta una copa" ("One Cup Short"). Upon checking her crystal, Eva finds that she has only eleven wine glasses left and decides to omit one of her customary twelve Christmas guests rather than have an unmatched service. She eliminates her nephew Fidel, whose widowed mother had died that year. Too shy to ask why he has not received an invitation, he is bewildered when he hears that others have. On Christmas night when the others inquire for him, she explains smoothly that he could not come. Fidel, eating Christmas dinner alone in a restaurant, continues examining his conscience, wondering what he had done wrong the previous year to prevent his being invited back. Despairing, he takes poison and dies at the restaurant table.

15. "Contra la pena" ("Pain Killers"). An old woman gives her granddaughter some candies to be eaten only when she is very sad, telling her that they have the wonderful quality of alleviating great pain. After the girl leaves, the grandmother takes one of the few candies she had retained to alleviate her own deep pain at the passing of another Christmas.

16. "Esta noche en Rusia" ("Tonight in Russia"). On Christmas a "travel-bureau-type" gentleman appears to Ramón in his study, and asks where he wishes to spend that Christmas. Ramón chooses Russia, and waits in his study that night until dark. When the lights come on, he finds himself in a sumptuous dining room where a couple, bemoaning the lagging arrival of their guests, decide to dine alone. Their dinner is interrupted when the doorbell is rung by a peasant and a forest guard who come to tell the host that they have found the frozen bodies of his strayed guests. He refuses to allow them to bring the bodies in, saying he had invited guests for supper and it is now after supper. He coolly advises them to take the corpses to the prefecture or the church, and he and his wife calmly have another drink. Then Ramón reawakens in his own study.

17. "Brindis de los dos viudos" ("The Widow and the Widower's Toast"). An elderly widow and widower, friends since their young married days, agree to meet secretly on Christmas night and finally enjoy the passion they have conscientiously stifled over the years. They dine, toast one another's dead spouses, and then she faints. He does too, apparently. When they awaken next morning, he very formally sees her out. Their toasts unexpectedly defeated the devil's plans in their regard.

18. "Ildefonso Cuadrado." A childless widower who has outlived all his friends and relatives, alone now on Christmas night, awaits the arrival of the Christmas card he has faithfully received from Ildefonso Cuadrado over the past fifteen or twenty years, and to which he has always replied. The doorbell rings, and, to his surprise, it is Cuadrado, who, after all these years, has finally come to call. He invites him to supper and inquires how he had started sending the cards. Cuadrado explains that one year, having twenty extra cards, he sent them to twenty people picked at random from the phone book. Each reply prompted another card the following year, until gradually, all dropped off but this one. Alone now, he had decided to make the acquaintance of his remaining correspondent. Both men realize their need for companionship and drink a succession of toasts until their cups break.

19. "Sin estar yo" ("Without My Being There"). Ramón here simply and nostalgically recalls a Christmas from his childhood.

20. "Epílogo" ("Epilogue"). When an extra page drops from his almanac, Ramón confesses his secret belief that there is always an extra day between December 31 and January 1, in which we all do things we cannot remember later.

The predominant and perhaps unifying element of this collection of stories is its element of nostalgia. Now sad, now tender, humorous or charming, all these stories share an element of nostalgia and simplicity that makes them seem almost like a collection of stories for children.

CHAPTER 5

Biography and Autobiography

I Evolution in the Biographical Works

RAMÓN Gómez de la Serna's first biographical works were interesting but not notable life stories. In them, although Ramón had clearly studied the lives and activities of his subjects and attempted to re-create them, the inimitable ramonesque qualities that appeared in his later biographical works were lacking.

His first biographical sketch, a study of Oscar Wilde, was published in *Prometeo* in 1911. His second, a study of Ruskin, appeared as an accompanying prologue for Carmen de Burgos' translation of Ruskin's *Stones of Venice* in 1913.

Then, in 1918, Ramón wrote a book about his own literary *tertulia*, which he entitled simply *Pombo*. In this work, he described the cafe itself, the feelings it inspired in him, and the nature and spirit of the gatherings held there. Believing that the essence of the Pombo *tertulia* was to be found in the wide variety of personalities comprised by its habitués, Ramón took pains to describe each of them in sketches which range from one or two paragraphs to several pages in length. In these sketches (frequently reminiscent of caricatures), Ramón early showed himself to be an excellent observer as he presented the salient elements of character, gesture, or appearance that most immediately conveyed the total impression created by his subjects. Manuel Abril's thin, sharp nose and nervous gestures, for example, brought forth the comment, "He looks like a flying wasp," while d'Ors's sedate bearing aroused comment on "his presidential manner of seating himself." Romero Calvet's black suits earned him the description: "Always in mourning, black like an owl."[1] A similar collection of sketches appeared in a second volume entitled *La sagrada cripta de Pombo (Pombo, the Sacred Crypt)*, which was published in 1924.

In the years between 1918 and 1924, Gómez de la Serna wrote a number of biographical prologues about foreign writers to accompany translations of their works by his brother Julio and by friends such as Ricardo Baeza and Mauricio Bacarisse. Although it is possible that Ramón wrote these early biographies largely because they were marketable, he nevertheless was able to exercise a certain selectivity over those he consented to write.

The predominance of French names (Baudelaire, Barbey d'Aurevilly, Villiers, Nerval, Remy de Gourmont) in these early biographical works attests to the writer's youthful enthrallment with Paris and the bizarre French bohemians about whom he had heard such colorful anecdotes. Similarly, his choice of Oscar Wilde as a subject was natural in a young man experiencing his first ardorous dedication to literature, for Ramón envisioned Wilde as a defiantly creative giant destroyed by the unyielding taboos of a bourgeois society.

Except for the sketch on Wilde, these early biographies are far from Ramón's best. Ruskin's comfortable English background, successful career, and socialistic experiments failed to fire his young biographer's imagination. Baudelaire, Barbey d'Aurevilly, Villiers, and Nerval, however, struggling with poverty, victimized by usurious editors, and rebelling against the society of their day, caught his fancy.

To some extent, the young biographer seems to have been influenced by his subjects. It is entirely possible that Villiers' habit of working through the night hours influenced the working regimen Ramón adopted for himself. Perhaps, too, it was Villiers' frustrated search for the ideal woman and his consequent decision to invent an artificial and perfect one which suggested Ramón's whimsical purchase of the life-size wax mannikin he kept with him in the *torreón* as his ideal woman. Possibly, also, it was Barbey d'Aurevilly's habit of writing in colored ink (particularly red) to dramatize the self-draining process of literary creation that influenced Ramón to adopt the same gesture. And it is quite likely that the capricious little sketches scattered throughout Barbey's writings gave Ramón the idea of scattering similar little sketches through works of his own, as he does in *Pombo, Autodeathography,* and the *Greguerías*.

When *Goya* appeared in 1928, it was a landmark in Ramón's biographical writing, for it added a quality Ramón's previous biographies had lacked: vitality. This biography of Goya was alive. Goya, to Ramón, was someone whose familiar influence had marked his formative years. His feeling for the artist had originated in childhood excursions through the Prado with his father, and continued through his adolescent years when he frequented that great museum, spending long hours contemplating Goya's paintings and studying the struggles and paradoxes, humor and drama, wry disillusionments and little ironies of life he saw depicted there. "Goya," he claimed, "was the school wherein I first realized what life was."[2]

The young writer felt an affinity with Goya, believing that, as the artist preserves life with his brush, so the writer records it with his pen. Quite possibly it was Goya's success in capturing the life of Madrid on canvas that impelled Ramón to capture it in writing and prompted books like *The Flea Market* (1915), *El Prado* (1920), *Madrid* (1920), *Toda la historia de la Puerta de Sol (The Complete History of the Puerta de Sol)*, 1925, and articles like "Toda la historia de la calle de Alcalá" ("The Complete History of Alcalá Street") and "Toda la historia de la Plaza Mayor" ("The Complete History of the Plaza Mayor") published in *La Tribuna*. The possibility of some relationship between Goya's *Caprichos* and Ramón's *greguerías* also arises, for Ramón is one of the first to comment on the aphoristic quality of the titles Goya bestowed on his *Caprichos*, describing them as "a contrast of the real with the imagined."[3] He saw in them a phantasmagoric element reaching almost to the point of surrealism and lingered over them in his biography of Goya, stressing their macabre elements and tragic humor which he felt reflected the artist's despair at the brevity and uncertainty of life. As Ramón himself matured, his own humor became increasingly tinged with pathos, and clownish behavior sometimes hid his own hunger or sadness. Thus, when he describes Goya, saying, "Though wounded, Goya still smiles,"[4] one cannot help wondering whether it is Goya he is describing, or himself, for in this biography, author and subject seem to have merged to such an extent that, as one critic has said, "his book has become almost an autobiography of Goya."[5]

A. *Azorín* (1930). Two years later, Ramón attained a second landmark in his biographical powers of evocation in *Azorín*. This book marks an evolution in Ramón's biographical style because of the unique collage technique by which it thrusts the reader into Azorín's world, skillfully presenting multiple facets of the Spanish scene in the first quarter of the twentieth century and showing Azorín's relation to it in such a way that his image emerges more completely and authentically than would have been possible in a more traditional biography. Gómez de la Serna presents Azorín in relation to his era, showing the vital circumstances surrounding and interacting with him to form his literary personality.

If the "little philosopher's" love of art, powers of observation, fondness for detail, and intense feeling for reality, the world of things, and the Flea Market endeared him to his biographer, his rejection of a legal or consular career so that he might pursue his literary vocation literally consecrated him. Unfortunately, Ramón later was disillusioned in his idol.[6] Basically, his disillusionment stemmed from the fact that the aging author had ceased writing and had become addicted to the movies. Humorist though he was, Ramón failed to see the humor in this.[7]

B. *Ismos (Isms)*, an interesting collection of partly biographical sketches, appeared in 1931, giving tangible proof of Gómez de la Serna's interest in the plastic arts and in the creative personalities of the artists who were most influential in establishing new trends. Written with imagination and humor, this book was a lighter work than one might expect. In it, Ramón presents a series of perceptive essay-type studies of literary and artistic movements which reveal both his knowledge of them and his intuitive powers of discernment. He expresses his belief that artists and writers share the creative and redeeming task of preserving "the light and shadow of their time,"[8] that they share the striving to detain death and to preserve life.[9]

Thus, in Picasso, for example, Gómez de la Serna saw an artistic expression of reality similar to that which he himself tried to achieve in writing; the superimposition of images and the juxtaposition of planes of reality. In Lhote, he saw a modified cubism. Cubism intrigued Ramón and he compared Apollinaire's effect on literature to that of cubism on painting.[10] Ramón wrote briefly of artists like the Delaunays and Marie Laurencin, and more at length on others whose more colorful personalities held greater interest for him, like Diego Rivera and Cocteau. Cocteau's work, both writing and painting, he baptized *Serafismo* for he said, "Everything in Cocteau's work requires a special velocity of contemplation."[11] *Isms* also contains a number of humorous "isms" of their author's own whimsical creation, like *Klaxismo* on the blowing of horns, *Botellismo* on the history and aesthetic selection of bottles, and *Jazzbandismo* on the musical phenomenon of the 1920's and 1930's.

C. *El Greco.* Much had changed in Ramón's life when he attained his next milestone in biographic achievement with the publication of *El*

Greco in 1935. Luisa, whom he loved with unreasonable possessiveness, lay at the point of death, and while keeping an anxious vigil at her side, Ramón worked feverishly on the manuscript whose publication he hoped would pay for the care and medicine she needed. In her semidarkened room surrounded by copies of El Greco's paintings, he wrote through the night. The resulting biography is permeated by an almost agonizing spirit of tension emphasized and reiterated throughout: tension between body and soul, mortality and immortality, the corporal and the spiritual, the earthly and the heavenly, the human and the divine. Ramón projects this interior tension as the very essence of Toledo and of El Greco, often with such feeling and such a deep concentration of poetic imagery that many passages read like prose poems.

This study seems to be another example of the *sinfronismo* mentioned by Ortega in which a subject from another era bridges the chasm of centuries, stimulates a latent feeling or germ of an idea in a contemporary soul, finds a radical affinity there, and through that soul achieves a new and fuller expression.[12] Rather than presenting a factual account of El Greco's life, Ramón re-creates his spirit, the atmosphere which surrounded, permeated, and enthralled him, and which was, in turn, perpetuated by him. Quite possibly because of the life-death struggle Luisa was undergoing while he was writing, Ramón arrived at an understanding of El Greco that he might not have attained at another time. The identification of self and subject so manifest in *Goya,* the blending of era and aura so skillfully combined to achieve the mood of an epoch in the collage-like presentation of *Azorín,* were welded together in the poetically subjective re-creation which emerged in *El Greco.*

II *Early Biographies in America*

Between the appearance of *El Greco* and Ramón's next biographical works, the Civil War erupted in Spain and Ramón emigrated to Argentina. The details of that emigration, the financial problems with which he had to contend, and the loneliness he experienced have been narrated in the chapter dealing with his life. In those first difficult years in Buenos Aires, Ramón's struggle to make ends meet kept him busy writing short articles for newspapers and magazines. Consequently, although Latin-American publishing houses reissued versions of his former works, few new ones appeared. In contrast with his former prolific production of new works, only one novel, five biographies, two volumes of biographical sketches, and two independently published sketches appeared in Ramón's first decade in America.[13] Of the biographies, the first three which appeared evinced little advance in Ramón's biographical art.

Mi tía, Carolina Coronado My Aunt, Carolina Coronado, 1940, seems to have been dictated primarily from a feeling of family pride in an aunt who had achieved literary renown as a poet. Ramón was not successful in his attempt to present her as the complete romantic, a figure of beauty and precocious talent, with powers of insight and premonition. Only the first chapter (literally an essay on the Romantic writers) in which he attempts to place her within the framework of her generation, has much general interest.

In 1943, Ramón produced *Velázquez,* a book which seems to be more a commentary on the artist's paintings than a study of his life and person. *Lope de Vega* appeared in 1945. Here, despite the fact that Ramó utilized excerpts from Lope's letters to the Duke of Sessa to provide authentic insights into his subject's life and personality, he also relied heavily upon arbitrary interpretations and inferences derived from Lope's plays and poems in re-creating his life. An augmented and revised edition of this biography appeared in 1954, entitled *Lope viviente (The Living Lope),* and Cardona Peña points out a glaring chronological error in it which reveals that Ramón was somewhat negligent in matters of chronology.[14] With a subject like Lope, so full of the zest of life and love, one wonders why Ramón failed to achieve the dynamic work which the revised title reveals that he intended.

The next three works which Ramón published were studies of contemporary artists. Two, "Maruja Mallo" (1942) and "Norah Borges" (1945), were published as preliminary studies to small volumes containing reproductions of the subject's paintings. The third, a book-length study, *José Gutiérrez Solana,* appeared in 1944. Here, reminiscing about the Pombo *tertulia* which Solana had immortalized in one of his most famous paintings, Ramón's fraternal feeling for the artist is evident. He recalls visits to the somber Solana household and tells of his subject's tendency to sing operatic arias in Pombo, in the family dining room, or even in the streets of Madrid when fortified by a few drinks. He stresses the solitude that marked the artist's life, a solitude intensified by the presence of his mentally ill mother in the home. Solana's personal integrity and his faith in his own art appealed to Ramón, as did the realistic qualities of his paintings. In the baroque morbidity pervading this artist's work, Ramón saw a relationship between him and Goya. He felt that, like Goya, Solana had captured the popular essence of Spain in his art.[15]

III Valle-Inclán

Ramón's biography of Valle-Inclán, which appeared in 1944, is one of his best biographical works. In it, the blend of humor and pathos growing in Ramón appears to have crystallized. The very title, *Don Ramón María del Valle-Inclán,* indicated the biographer's respect for his subject, and the work reveals the warm affection he felt for the inimitable, indomitable, and extravagant spirit he saw beneath his subject's skinny frame and stringy beard. Ramón's "gregueristic" spirit reveled in the abundance of colorful anecdotes circulating about Valle and he freely invented still others to show his subject's aggressive, volatile personality. The anecdotes (so much a part of Valle that even in his lifetime writers were paid by newspapers for submitting plausible-sounding ones for publication) assume a primary importance in this biography.

From adolescence, Gómez de la Serna had admired the obdurate Galician, seeing in him the perfect bohemian, one who blended life and literature so completely that he created a true literary personality for himself. As a creative artist, Valle-Inclán embodied many of the ideals closest to Ramón's heart. He was incorruptible, independent, uncompromising, dedicated, proud, and poor — a true artist-creator, all of which earned him the right to act and be treated as a superior being. Besides this, everything else in his life — poverty, hunger, humiliation — paled into insignificance. Ramón shows him wearing his poverty proudly, almost as a badge of independence, and describes the effect this had upon him, personally, saying, "I who have felt myself badly humiliated and embarrassed beside so many men, alongside Valle-Inclán, felt proud, happy as if in the company of an extremely distinguished personage."[16] Ramón lamented the public's lack of appreciation for the eccentric Galician. His subject's prodigious fecundity and originality fascinated him and he admired and imitated Valle's free use of fantasy. Fernández Almagro notes that Gómez de la Serna launched his *Disparates (Absurdities)* about the same time that Valle-Inclán wrote his first *Esperpentos,* and speculates upon the possible influence Valle-Inclán may have had upon his biographer's work.[17]

Gómez de la Serna shared his subject's inclination toward juxtaposing the basic elements of tears and laughter, life and death, and his masterful biography reveals this, showing Valle's vibrantly alive, creative spirit side by side with his poverty, hunger, lack of appreciation, and abandonment. The hardships Valle endured in persevering in his literary vocation made him seem a veritable martyr to Ramón and caused him to declare that he saw something Christlike in his subject.[18] Valle, not unaware of the younger author's admiration, at his death requested that Ramón be his biographer.

IV *Biographical Sketches*

Perhaps it was the loneliness of the emigré that turned Ramón's thoughts back to the other writers he had known in Spain; perhaps the upheaval of the Civil War made him realize the importance of his era and the men who had formed it; or perhaps he was influenced more than he realized by Ortega's theory of man and his circumstances. Whatever the reason, Ramón availed himself of his new circumstances and vantage point in America to look more objectively upon the world of men that had surrounded him in Spain, reexamine it, and seek to penetrate its meaning. In the process, he produced two noteworthy volumes of biographical sketches: *Retratos contemporáneos, (Contemporary Portraits),* 1941 and *Nuevos retratos contemporáneos (New Contemporary Portraits),* 1945.

When he prepared *Contemporary Portraits* for publication, Ramón included revisions of sketches of Girondo, Cassau, Vighi, Ruiz Contreras, Carrere, Hoyos, and d'Ors (Zenius), that he had published earlier in *Pombo;* of Morand, Remy de Gourmont, and Colette that were printed as prologues; of Baroja, Unamuno, and Valle-Inclán that had appeared in the biography of Azorín, and one of Natalia Barney that had appeared independently, as an article. The rest were new. In *Nuevos retratos contemporáneos* (New Contemporary Portraits), only the sketch of Cansinos Asséns had appeared previously (in *Pombo,* I). The subjects Ramón selected for his *retratos* were writers, musicians, or painters who had not appeared in *Ismos.* The sketches in both volumes had two qualities in common: (1) all the subjects were in some way creative artists who stood out in relation to their contemporaries; and (2) almost all, at some time or other in their lives, had been in personal contact with Ramón. For purposes of study, it seems expedient to consider the sketches together, rather than as two separate bodies, and to group them according to Ramón's treatment of their subjects.

Gómez de la Serna's selection of subjects was a very arbitrary one, as he himself realized. Ramón seemed to enjoy the capricious disparity of his subjects, rationalizing that precisely such disparity provides the key to a literary period.[19] In this group, the subjects were not idols to Ramón, but contemporaries, and his feelings for

Biography

them were not tinged with awe, but with the personal affection or disaffection he felt for confreres engaged in the same pursuit of creative and artistic expression as he was. He wished simply to present intimate and truthful glimpses of his subjects as he had known them.

"I saw them all full length, without allowing myself to be taken in by their affectations, yet pinpointing the special qualities with which they embraced a literary career.... It seems to me that biography is the best interpretation of the soul and work of an author."[20] These words of Ramón's reveal that, for him, biography was a means of interpreting his subjects' lives and works; his end was to arrive at a sincere literary judgment.

His sketches were of dissimilar men who had affected him differently. Most were cherished friends, but some were men and women whom he disliked. Consequently, they may be grouped into two general classifications: affirmative or negative, depending upon whether or not the subject conformed to the aesthetic and ethical norms Ramón maintained for the artist-creator.

V   *Affirmative Sketches*

Perhaps Ramón's sketches of Oliverio Girondo, Vighi, Cami, Bontempelli, Pitigrilli, Villalón, and Carrère are the most noticeably cordial in their expression of warm personal friendship. His friendships with Girondo, Vighi, and Carrère were of long standing, and their portraits had been included in the first volume of *Pombo* (1918). Girondo, like Ramón, combined interests in both art and literature, had a gift for audacious metaphor, and possessed the personal qualities of creativity, innovation, and persistent bohemianism. His *Espantapájaros (Scarecrow)* had been ignored by critics much as had Ramón's *The Flea Market,* and Ramón felt the injustice of both slights. Like Ramón, however, Girondo kept faith with literature and continued to see life and men with chaplinesque humor.

Vighi had been a childhood friend of Ramón's as well as a *pombiano*. In evoking Vighi, Ramón re-creates the scene of his entrance into Pombo on any typical Saturday night, portrays his buoyant good nature, the teasing he received from the group, and even records some of the amusing original poems he read. Similarly, Ramón's portrayal of Cami emerges as an affectionate testimonial of the good times they enjoyed together in Paris at the French Academy of Humor, and of high-spirited attempts they made at literary collaboration with Pitigrilli.

Mac-Orlan, Noel, and García Calderón, with their colorful

bohemianism, also struck a responsive chord in Ramón. Their sketches reflect the admiration he felt at their courage in departing from the conventional as well as his sorrow at the obstacles an uncomprehending society placed in their way. In writing of Noel, Ramón reveals a personal sorrow for the dire poverty in which the eccentric writer lived, and for the terrible frustration which public indifference caused in his creative spirit.

Similarly, Ramón's biography of Macedonio Fernández bears witness to his enormous empathy for the aging writer's belief in himself and in his work, and to the sorrow he experienced because of the other's continued failure to attain recognition. In stressing the perceptive observation of reality that led his subject to a reality beyond the present one, Ramón indirectly gives us a key to his own attitude toward reality, commenting, "This serious ingenuity . . . is the utmost a writer can attain, as far as I am concerned."[21] His empathy for his subject also had a personal basis, for he confessed: "Now that I am also living in . . . Argentina . . . I understand better the martyrdom and aloneness he had to suffer in the spiritually lonely roads of his persistence."[22]

In much the same vein, Ramón decried Kafka's suffering of the tragedy of "discouragement, neglect, defeat, forms which, more than penury, are what I consider the 'misery' of a poet."[23] He felt that Kafka not only exceeded the limits of reality, but even used reality to surpass reality. He payed tribute to Kafka's unwavering devotion to the literary ideal, saying, "His manuscripts . . . were made and paid for, paid for with his life."[24]

When Ramón perceived in another a kindred striving to attain the literary ideal as he did, for example, in Paul Morand, Enrique Larreta, Enrique de Mesa, and Ibsen, he felt a deep affinity with that person. "We are united by the same appetite for the ideal," he says of Larreta,[25] and of Morand: "We recognized in one another the same traces of intellectual suffering. . . . We succored one another with our smiles."[26] Despite the fact that Enrique de Mesa, with his love for the classics, followed a different ideal than Ramón's innovative one, Ramón nevertheless respected his sincerity and perseverance and described him as "a quixotic figure who enlivened letters for more than thirty years."[27] Of Ibsen, whom he considered a magnificent idealist, Ramón said, "He aspired to the pinnacle and persisted in his thirst for the ideal."[28] He respected Ibsen's spirit of complete dedication and the solitary life he lived in pursuit of his literary ideal.

The loneliness so often inherent in the life of a creative personality intrigued Ramón.[29] He notes it in many of his biographies and makes special mention of it in those on Saint-Paul Roux, Ibsen, Macedonio Fernández, Kafka, Remy de Gourmont, Miró, Falla, and Colette. In his biography of Colette, solitude becomes a major theme and forms almost the basis of his study.

The need of the creative person for free and independent personal expression also impressed Ramón. In his sketch on Keyserling, he praises him for propounding this theory. In Unamuno, Ramón found that the struggle for uncompromising, independent expression existed on both an artistic and a personal plane. Referring to his subject's strivings he writes, "The novelistic life of Unamuno is pure struggle, the fertile struggle of novelty. . . ."[30] Alluding to Unamuno's personal and moral conduct, he says "He always did what he thought he should do, without thinking of the consequences. . . . He never commited the enormous sin of keeping still."[31] In his biography of Miró, Ramón reveals that he esteemed and respected his subject both for his artistic ability and for his faithful adherence to his own mode of expression. Recalling his own efforts at persuading Miró to undertake newspaper or magazine writing to supplement his income, Ramón tells how Miró repulsed the suggestion, for fear that periodical writing would affect the meticulousness of his style.[32]

Frequently, it was as much the literary style of a subject as his personal qualities that made Ramón feel an inner kinship with him. A striking example of this may be seen in his arbitrary inclusion of Bartrina (a poet who had died in 1880) in *New Portraits* purely because "He has always attracted me. . . . I feel him as if he were my most intimate contemporary."[33] He considered Bartrina "a great, disconcerting and original poet"[34] who belonged more to the vanguard of the contemporary generation than to his own period. Bartrina's sardonic humor appealed to Ramón, as did the brief Campoamor-like poems which he called "Arabescos" and "Intimas."[35]

In his sketch of Neruda, Ramón points out the poet's extraordinary metaphors, his sensitivity to things, and his intense appreciation of reality. The common ground shared with Pedro de Répide was a quality of reality — his absorbing interest in Madrid — that gave Ramón a feeling of kinship for him. Madrid was the constant theme of Répide's articles, books, and theatrical works. "If anyone has adorned the streets of Madrid with sympathy, intellect, and chasteness it has been Pedro de Répide," wrote Ramón.[36] A number of Ramón's biographical sketches deal with eccentric figures, a type that never failed to intrigue him. The dauntless impertinence of a colorful personality like George Bernard Shaw delighted Ramón. He did not understand Shaw, but he did appreciate the literary personality he had constructed. Shaw, however, lacked an essential quality that Ramón looked for in the literary man: he was not essentially a poet.[37] Similarly, the man-hating Natalia Barney, the picaresque Pijoán, and the mysterious Ilya Ehrenburg, all fascinated Ramón and were re-created in his sketches.

VI *Negative Sketches*

Not all of Gómez de la Serna's sketches were as full of empathic appreciation as the preceding ones. A number of revered literary figures of both the nineteenth and twentieth centuries received censure in them. The intensity of his negative attitudes varied with his subjects. For some, he had mixed feelings of admiration and reproof; for others, mild disapproval; for still others, virtual contempt. It is perhaps easier to consider Ramón's negative sketches in order of intensity rather than in chronological order. As a biographer, Ramón enjoyed and noted his subject's eccentricities. When he wrote of Juan Ramón Jiménez, for instance, his subject's abhorrence of noise, his arbitrary creation of a literary personality, and his predilection for the letter "J" were all duly noted. "The worst of all errors is to call him Giménez instead of Jiménez," Ramón said; "He will never pardon it."[38] As a confrere, Ramón concedes his subject's poetic greatness. He appreciated his chimeric evocations, his masterly use of imagery, his expressionistic treatment of landscape. He even affirmed that "*Platero y yo* was born immortal."[39] However, like everyone else who knew the poet from Moguer, Ramón found his excessive pride irritating, and complained of it. Jiménez' touchiness was also difficult to contend with, and Ramón confessed, "I decrease my visits to the poet because it is difficult to speak with him."[40] Another thing that Ramón found difficult to accept was that Juan Ramón allowed his wife to supplement their income by arranging foreign student exchanges and housing. To Gómez de la Serna it seemed demeaning and unworthy for a man of literature to be so mercenary.

Eugenio d'Ors, too, fell short of Ramón's ideal, failing in his artistic, rather than his personal, integrity. Ramón felt that, in his search for ease and comfort, d'Ors had never realized his creative potential. He did, however admire his subject's personal integrity, and praised the courage d'Ors had revealed in speaking out when frank speech was not popular in Spain.

Ramón's sketch of Pardo Bazán conveys his impression of a comfortably situated woman of mediocre talent, willing to grind out mediocre works upon demand. Somewhat similarly, Ramón describes Pérez Galdós as lacking in artistic and creative powers. He attributes the interest aroused by the *Episodios nacionales* not to Galdós' writing, but to the interest inherent in the historical episodes themselves. In this study, Ramón's resentment at the economic success of a writer he considered mediocre is obvious. And in his sketch of Pío Baroja, our biographer reveals that the brusque Basque both attracted and exasperated him. He concedes Baroja's gift for realistic writing, yet denies that he had any artistic qualities. He expresses chagrin at Baroja's admittance to the Spanish Academy, justifying his harshness toward Baroja somewhat illogically by citing Baroja's own harshness toward others.[41]

Cansinos Asséns received short shrift from Ramón — despite the fact that his sketch in *Portraits* was intended to modify earlier, harsher sketches that had appeared in both volumes of *Pombo*. Here, Ramón indicates that Cansinos countered his refusal to convert Pombo into the nucleus of a new literary movement by forming a *tertulia* of his own at the Cafe Colonial which encouraged the "Ultraist" movement. Ramón infers that this was the final act which caused him and his cohorts to drop Cansinos.

Gómez de la Serna's portrayal of Ruiz Contreras is more a caricature than a biographical sketch. In it he unflatteringly shows how Ruiz Contreras' eccentricities and avarice increased with age. Yet, because the old man had been instrumental in encouraging and aiding young writers in his days as editor of the *Biblioteca Nueva* press and the *Revista Nueva*, Ramón is kinder in his treatment of him than of Baroja or Cansinos Asséns.

A predominantly negative tone marks Ramón's sketch of Benavente. Although he praised his subject's wit, ingenuity, sincerity, and modesty, Ramón nevertheless mocked his enormous popularity, saying: "He was . . . the favorite of grandparents."[42] When *New Portraits* appeared in print, Benavente wrote an article in a Barcelona newspaper denying the truth of some of the anecdotes Ramón had ascribed to him in his sketch. Ramón promptly replied with a stinging countercorrection in the same paper. Years later, in *Nuevas páginas de mi vida (New Pages of My Life)*, when he expresses his belief that Benavente's *El príncipe que todo aprendió en los libros* had been plagiarized from his own *Cuento de Calleja (Alley Tale)*, which he had given Benavente to read, Ramón's irritation is clarified.[43]

Blasco Ibáñez too, is criticized quite negatively. Although Ramón did not deny his subject's artistic ability, his sketch indicates resentment at Blasco's financial success that, to him, implies a lack of personal integrity. Blasco had promised Spain's writers that he would establish a Spanish Academy for them similar to the French Academie Goncourt, complete with endowment and annual stipend. He promised to leave his chalet, too, as a rest home for them. None of this, Ramón notes almost bitterly, ever materialized.

The antithesis of all Gómez de la Serna's ideals seems to have been embodied in Echegaray. Like many other Spanish writers, Ramón was outraged when Echegaray was awarded the Nobel Prize for literature. Don José lived a correct and comfortable life; he did not suffer poverty, neglect, nor abandonment; he was not creative, but traditional. Ramón insists that he was not an artist, but an engineer, and infers that he was not even a good engineer. He comments, bitingly, that "men of science consider him a 'great dramatist' and literary men consider him a 'great mathematician.' "[44]

From a survey of Ramón's negative sketches, it becomes apparent that his unfavorable attitudes toward their subjects derived either from his personal disapproval of their personal qualities, of their literary production, or both. The personal qualities he censured were desire for monetary gain, disloyalty to friends or ideals, and lack of total dedication to the creative task. The literary sins he excoriated were mediocrity (lack of creative or artistic qualities), plagiarism, and desecration of the literary ideal for monetary gain.

VII *Interrelationship of Ramon's Biographical and Autobiographical Writing*

The appearance of the two volumes of portraits apparently marked the necessary and final steps in Ramón's progress toward the writing of his own autobiography. In the prologue of *Portraits,* he had written, "After writing all the biographies remaining, I shall write my autobiography, which I am secretly working on and it will be utterly sincere."[45] It is a remark which leads one to consider the possible relation between Ramón's biographical sketches and his *Autodeathography*. After studying Ramón's biographical writings, his cousin, Gaspar Gómez de la Serna, came to the conclusion that, in them, Ramón ". . . exercises himself exploring human life, his own, and those of others, . . . writers and artists like himself, . . . whose outlines become mirrors of his own life."[46] Even a cursory reading of these works confirms this. Quite possibly, while working

Biography [113]

on his biographies of others, Ramón would turn occasionally to the manuscript of his own autobiography and add, delete, or color parts referring to those in hand. Many of his subjects had appeared previously, in relation to him, in an earlier version of his autobiography incorporated into *Pombo, Vol. II,* which narrated his life up to the period when he lived at Estoril. Now, reconsidering these former associates and their relationships with him with the greater wisdom and perception that his distance from Spain and his maturer vision gave him, Ramón came both to understand them better and to know himself more profoundly. It was as if he had caught numerous partial glimpses of himself and his life reflected in each life that he studied, and, by assembling these fragmentary glimpses, ultimately arrived at a truer, fuller concept of himself. As Gaspar Gómez de la Serna states, "Each one of these men, is, in certain measure, another self for Ramón . . . mirrors in the depths of whose combined refraction appears Ramón himself."[47]

As Gómez de la Serna noted, autobiographical parts are to be found in many of Ramón's other works, both biographical and fictional. The more one reads of Ramón's works, the more apparent does it become that in all he wrote, he delineated himself. Gómez de la Serna commented that in Ramón's biographical studies, he "adds to his literary documentation . . . his own testimonial of the times . . . the problems . . . conditioning their common lives."[48] Ramón seemed almost to attempt living the biographies he wrote in much the same manner in which an actor, representing a character on stage, infuses his own soul into that of the person he portrays, identifying with him so completely and intensely that he becomes that character. Like such a performance, Ramón's biographies exceed the limits of mere portrayal and become a means of self-expression. Time after time in his biographical writing, one encounters lines that are unabashedly self-expressive as the hopes, dreams, sorrows, and protests of Ramón's subjects fuse with his own.

In his biography of Wilde, for example, he laments: "There is an abject pleasure for most people in seeing a great man fallen, ostracized, or mistreated. It seems as if this brings him down to their size."[49] In the *Autodeathography* he reiterates: "The writer is a being whose hungers, loves and dishonors alone acquire great publicity."[50] In Lope's biography he complains: "The misery of the Spanish writer is proverbial."[51] Ramón, it becomes apparent, had consistently and indirectly been working on his own autobiography while he wrote his biographical works. Finally, in 1948, it appeared, a mammoth volume of almost nine hundred pages, bearing the curious title *Automoribundia (Autodeathography)*. Its title, he explained, indicated that it was "the story of how a man progresses toward death."[52]

VIII Autodeathography

In *Autodeathography*, Ramón purported to tell, once and for all, the intimate truths of his life and to correct previous deliberate misinformation. "In other autobiographical sketches, I have lied," he admitted, "but now, on writing my definitive autobiography, I do not wish to begin by lying."[53]

He begins this "veridical" story by describing the day of his birth, July 3, 1888:

> The first thing that I did was to pee. . . . While I did that I stretched comically, much as does a duck when he breaks out of the egg. . . . The lights bothered my eyes so much I did not want to open them. They bathed me and I felt better, although exhausted, and I continued stretching my head, arms, and legs to get the stiffness out of them.[54]

In this life story, Ramón admits disarmingly, "It is so difficult to avoid invention and false anecdote."[55] Essentially artistic and creative, he wrote autobiography in much the same way that he had written biography — which means that he sometimes invented facts to project ideas he considered vital. Essentially a humorist, he utilized humor in a unique way, making of it a device through which to obtain new perspectives on life, reach into the depths of the subconscious, and attain the heights of the surreal. In his desire to be known wholly and utterly, he sought to record not merely the vital statistics of his life, but also the events, hopes, dreams, aches, illusions, and fantasies of his waking and dreaming hours. Alternating between pathos and humor, *Autodeathography* was a sincere attempt by the author to tell the intimate story of his life in his own inimitable manner.

As the title indicates, the idea of "living toward death" is fundamental in Ramón. It was revealed in his fondness for the portrait of "The living-dead woman" he kept in his study, in his predilection for the morbid paintings of Goya, and in his appreciation for the macabre works of Solana. It brought about his intense consciousness of the simple wonder of being alive and his eagerness to explore and record every facet of life in its entirety to prevent its being irreparably lost. To record these thoughts and things important to him, Ramón utilized the essay, hence his autobiography is replete with essays on a variety of subjects. There are essays on faith in God, reality, the circus, pipesmoking, the parts of his body, poverty, Christmas, things, banks and checks, dinners, illness, summer, bohemianism, spikenards, and women, to mention only a few.

The foolish-looking little cartoons and pictures of himself which Ramón scattered throughout the *Autodeathography* should not be overlooked, for they reflect a hunger for recognition that characterized him all his life and seemed almost to be a way of crying aloud for notice. Despite the fact that his belief in himself, his work, his creativity, and his *greguerías* never wavered, Ramón nevertheless felt strongly that he had never received the recognition he merited. His chapter on nails, for example, seems to reflect the deep anxiety he felt to make his mark. Similarly, he treasured every word of homage paid to him at banquets and in critical reviews, and incorporated them into his autobiography or into the appendix that accompanies it.

Frustrated and saddened because the literary world never acknowledged him as the precursor he knew himself to be, Ramón ascribed this lack of comprehension to envy. It seems indeed likely that, in many ways, Ramón was ahead of his time, and a lapse of time is often required for the appreciation of any work. It is only today that critics and readers are beginning to comprehend and appreciate the deliberate lack of coherence, juxtaposition of planes, and the paradoxically serious humor that Ramón attempted (and achieved) in novels like *The Incongruent One* and in biographies like *El Greco, Poe,* and *Quevedo.*

Part of the appeal of Ramón's *Autodeathography* lies in the paradoxical quality which is its essence. Basically, it is the tragic story of a great humorist, a story told earnestly and sincerely by a man who unfalteringly believed in himself, yet felt rejected and unappreciated by the men of his own time. It is the story of a man's life written as fully as he could write it, in the hope that a later generation might know and understand him as he truly was and appreciate the creative endeavor of his life. This is autobiography in a new sense. All that Ramón had written before, every method of re-creation and self-expression that he had learned previously, every aspect of truth or variation of perspective learned in his previous works is brought into play here. In *Autodeathography,* Ramón has utilized humor, essay, narrative, anecdote, dialogue, *greguería,* paradox, and a great many varieties of rhetorical image to lay bare the innermost recesses of his mind, heart, and soul, and to portray, in very truth, "the story of how a man progresses toward death."[56]

IX *After* Autodeathography: Poe *and* Quevedo

Ramón's self-expression through his subjects reached a high point in the two masterly biographies that followed the appearance of *Autodeathography: Edgar Poe, genio de América (Edgar Poe, the Genius of America)* and *Quevedo,* both published in 1953. They were written by a man deeply wounded by the coolness that had marred the final part of his return trip to Spain in 1949, and who was still laboring under the financial strain that the trip had caused him. The appearance of these two biographies brought him the first financial relief he had known since that voyage. The increased bitterness evident in these works is therefore understandable. Ramón's indignation at and empathy for the poverty endured by the truly dedicated artist-creator reached new extremes in *Poe.*

As a subject, Poe fits all Ramón's ideals: he lived a bohemian life, combining dedication to the literary ideal with a veritable martyrdom of poverty and hardship; he had wonderfully fantastic powers of invention and a dramatic life story. Ramón had published an earlier version of his *Poe* in 1920, but more than thirty years later, after he, too, had lived in the New World, Ramón felt that he understood Poe better and revised his biography. The revised edition revealed the extraordinary poetic level of expression Ramón had by then attained.

In *Quevedo,* it seems that the quality that most appealed to Ramón was his subject's love for expressing the unvarnished truth. Quevedo's biography is characterized by a baroque piling of metaphor upon metaphor and *greguería* upon *greguería.* In it, Ramón "becomes" Quevedo to such an extent that he even paraphrases him. He considers Quevedo's laugh essential to him, and cleverly plays upon it. In these biographical works, Ramón taught himself to laugh with the laugh of Quevedo and to dream surrealistic dreams with the fantastic imagination of Poe. He made of these two figures (as he had of other subjects from the past) living and contemporary personalities. The contemporaneity which Ramón felt with artists who had lived in the past is party explicable by his belief that a similarity exists between the past and present experience of life.[57]

X *Humor and Vital Perspectives*

Something more than contemporaneity and identification marks these last works, however, particularly *Quevedo.* The humor Ramón had cultivated all his life became increasingly tinged with pathos as he grew older, and its blending with sadness, so evident before (particularly in his biographies of *Goya, Solana, Valle-Inclán* and the *Autodeathography*), became dominant now, enabling him to open up new perspectives through which to look at life. The more intensely absorbed Ramón became by the vital process of life, the more serious his humor became. Cardona has observed that "for Ramón the extreme seriousness of life must be treated lightly. This is his ultimate paradox."[58] He compares Ramón's melancholy humor with Chaplin's, and suggests that both are so constantly aware of death that they are terribly aware of being alive. As Ramón wrote in his *Autodeathography:* "The humorist takes for his own the maxim that life is something so serious that one must take it in jest. That is why excessive sadness . . . arrives at the superation of pain which is laughter."[59] There is an essential parallelism between Chaplin's humor and Ramón's. Cardona, observing it, wrote:

> Their basic concepts of humor are alike. The paradox of humor — that the humorist is the most serious man in the world — is perhaps what gives Ramón and Chaplin the same kind of greatness. . . . The greatest paradox of the mind is the mind's own desire to discover something it cannot think. The greatest paradox of Ramón's and Chaplin's mind is their desire to express something that cannot be expressed, namely, the overwhelming seriousness of life, which being so, one must, paradoxically, think of it as a joke. . . . They are magnificent exponents of a humor which penetrates into the depths of human sensitivity.[60]

XI Final Autobiographical Works

After *Autodeathography,* in addition to the biographies of Poe and Quevedo, three additional works of an autobiographical nature brought Ramón's long labor of life-writing to a close: *Cartas a las golondrinas (Letters to the Swallows),* 1949, *Cartas a mí mismo (Letters to Myself),* 1956, and *Nuevas páginas de mi vida (New Pages of My Life),* 1957. The first may be said to be autobiographical only in the sense that any book of essays on the author's random thoughts is autobiographical. In it, Ramón has written on topics suggested by the flight of the swallows: serenity, sincerity, the ephemeral quality of adolescence, of life, and so forth.

The second work, however, *Letters to Myself,* is more truly autobiographical in nature, for as the aging Ramón found himself increasingly abandoned and forgotten, he turned to writing letters to himself. The humor that appears in these letters is tremulous. Life's final tragedies of old age, poverty, abandonment, and illness bring only sad smiles or mournful jest to the old humorist. In this work, lines like the following, touched with pathos, abound:

It is an embarrassment of loneliness to have to write to you ... there are ever fewer people to write to ... for no one answers.[61]

To whom shall I write letter after letter if you are the only one in the world?[62]

I have no appointments with anyone this week, or the next, or the following ...[63]

I began to write these letters to you in jest, but as the days pass, I write them in earnest, and such earnestness frightens even me.[64]

You will be surprised at this letter in which I shall ask for money ... only of you am I not ashamed to ask.[65]

This letter satisfies me and provides me an outlet.[66]

The third book in this group, *New Pages of My Life,* serves almost as an epilogue to Ramón's writings. In his biographical works, Ramón had invariably added epilogues — sometimes several. It could hardly be expected then, that having survived *Autodeathography,* he would allow the record of his life to end there. He had anticipated this and concluded that voluminous work with the words: "Everything said in this book is valid until today, June 10, 1948, the day on which I begin writing an even more sincere and scandalous book which will be entitled, 'What I did not say in my *Automoribundia.'* "[67]

In *New Pages* Ramón explained the addition of these pages saying, "Life, like those collections of encyclopedic dictionaries, needs many appendices."[68] This book serves almost as a summary and synthesis of all that Ramón has said before. In it, he recapitulates his concept of the artist-creator's vocation:

A dispenser of his soul and a violinist of himself, the writer-artist is one who cannot change his destiny or profession.[69]

A writer seeks the truth. . . . His mission is very complicated, for, besides writing the truth, he has to write ... as if to remember things he never knew.[70]

Biography

Miners of themselves, they present the reader with that which cost them so much to tear from the depths of their own mines. Their torture is voluntary and lonely.[71]

In this work, Ramón divulges facts he had previously withheld. Now, for example, he expresses openly the plagiarism he had formerly merely hinted at in Benavente, saying: "I could not go to the next world without relating this incident of credulity and disillusionment."[72] He summarizes his position before life with the words: "Pervading all my comments is an affectionate vision of the world and its hardships, for my motto is that it is better to have a happy heart than a happy life, for a happy heart makes up for everything."[73] At sixty-eight, Ramón was painfully aware that life was passing. The best part of his years was behind him, and looking back, he felt that life on the whole had not been so bad. Despite his many misfortunes, life, he concluded, was beautiful.[74]

As he approached life's end, however, Ramón attempted to establish a position that would endure beyond it. He had returned to the practice of his religion in 1954, and he found consolation in that now, saying, "The man with a soul exists not just in time, but in eternity. Men who believe they have no souls exist only in time."[75] He reflects on the essence of immortality: "Immortality is composed of something other than time, a plenitude of sensibility more than of space."[76]

In one of the final pages of this last autobiographical work, the aging and lonely writer, who all his life had yearned for the recognition he sincerely and intensely felt he merited, wrote: "I am more determined than ever that what I am and what I always wanted should not be forgotten. It is my only fortune and I wish to save it."[77] These words sound a final plea for understanding. All his life Ramón had struggled quixotically to find and express the essential truth of his being.

It is noteworthy then, that in the trajectory of Gómez de la Serna's biographical works, the reader makes the same artistic and literary friends and acquaintances as did Ramón, and is led by the biographer himself along the same route he had traveled in his journey of self-discovery, self-revelation, self-expression, and self-preservation. Much as he might have led his reader through the Flea Market of Madrid, Ramón has led him through a sort of biographical *Rastro*. In each biography he has given his reader insights into his own life and personality. The accumulation of these myriad partial insights and fragments of information eventually comes to form a composite portrait of their creator.

CHAPTER 6

Unpublished Works

A STUDY of the papers left by Ramón Gómez de la Serna when he died reveals not only a number of incomplete or projected works, but also his method of composition.[1] It shows that he apparently did not write "manuscripts" until his works were well under way. His effects included numerous folders crammed with loose, yellow, approximately 3 x 5 and 5 x 8 slips of paper on which he recorded in red ink his random thoughts, flashes of intuition, and spontaneous or metaphoric associations. Their size seems to indicate that he kept them always within easy reach, perhaps even in his pockets.[2] These countless, tiny notes, sometimes misspelled, often lacking accents or punctuation, indicate by the varying degrees of legibility and illegibility of their scrawl that they were written either hurriedly, or when their author was tired, sleepy, ill, or perhaps even intoxicated.[3] They provide an unusual opportunity to study the creative process of a writer.

From them, it seems that Ramón made multitudinous random notes, later labeled them in the upper left-hand corner indicating their subject matter, and eventually sorted them into folders which he made from the backs of old books whose pages he had torn out. These "binders," on which he patiently printed his subject by pen, are simply bound with rubber bands. Apparently, when a binder came to contain ample material for an article, a study, or a book, Ramón sifted, sorted, and rearranged his yellow slips of paper, numbered them in the upper right corner, and used them as a basis from which to write his manuscripts.

In addition to these yellow notepapers, his binders also contained clippings of jokes, picturesque phrases, and parts of articles by others, culled from a miscellany of sources, as well as copies of his own published or typewritten articles. From the notations on his articles, it is evident that Ramón reworked them, changing titles, reorganizing content, altering, adding or deleting material, in order to use them for more than one publication.

The genesis of his biographical works may also be surmised from a study of these folders. From them it becomes apparent that Ramón's "research" consisted basically of scrapbook-like collections of items about his subjects. In folders labeled, for example, "Unamuno" or "Ortega," one finds numerous clippings of biographical articles by other authors culled from miscellaneous sources such as newspapers and magazines, and even whole biographical chapters torn from books; there are photos and sketches (originals, or reproductions clipped from newspapers or magazines) of the subjects, their parents, families, homes, and so on; clippings from their works, clippings of articles about them or their works, numerous slips of Ramón's typical 3 x 5 yellow notepaper with jottings of first- and second-hand impressions about his subject's works, lives or persons, even clippings of necrological articles — in short, everything pertinent to his subjects that came to his attention. Evidently, after collecting sufficient material to form a clear impression of his subject, Ramón reread it to refresh his memory, revive his impressions, and stimulate his imagination, and only then began to write his own subjective, impressionistic, and suprisingly "original" biography.

Ramón left a number of such projects unfinished when he died. Some binders apparently contain embryonic novels, dramas, plot outlines or ideas, possible titles for future works, and even what appear to be projected full-length biographical studies of Unamuno and Ortega. Examples of other projected works indicated by the binders are: "Dictionary Notes," "Explanation of Buenos Aires," "The Zoo," "Ballet and Cabaret," "Correcting Portraits" (presumably, rectifications, meant to modify previously published biographical sketches), "Time and Clocks," "Perspectives of Spain," "Editors," and even "God."

Aside from the two projected biographical works mentioned above, the four most advanced, and consequently, most interesting binders are those on "Dictionary Notes," "Spain," "Editors," and "God." From the approximately 750 notations on definitions or usage labeled "Dictionary Notes," it appears that Ramón intended to write a dictionary of witty and ingenious definitions, neologisms and "pseudo" words. The following sample conveys the tenor of the projected work:

FILICIDE	The murder of one's child.
GLACIOLOGIST	One who studies ice at the poles.
HOMOLANDIA	Perversionapolis.
PREDECEASED	One who dies before another. The opposite of survivor.
TRACTIONIST	One who drives a tractor.
VELAZQUEZ	Greyblue, poise and aristocratic profiles.

Ramón's projected work on "Editors," was, apparently, to be written in quite another vein. These notes reflect his many unfortunate experiences with editors in his later years. As the sampling below indicates, they are notes full of pathos, self-pity, and constantly reiterated plaints of poverty, frustration, and abuse:

I have no literary problems other than those with editors — of knowing whether or not they will accept my work, delay it, or having promised publication, not comply.

I believe I have not written all the works I could have written because I have not had guaranteed editors waiting for anything that came from my pen. They all expected "such and such a thing, and not something else."

An editor can have the vile privilege of trying to strangle a writer.

They want to see us suffer, become poor, earn the little that, by law, filters through their hands. . . .

Editor . . . the great procurer, who, for money alone lends himself to presenting the mediocre. . . .

There are some editors who aren't happy unless they know that some, who could have been writers, had it occurred to them to launch them, are dying of hunger, of impotence, of unpublished works. . . .

"Perspectivas de España" ("Perspectives of Spain") or "Ida y vuelta a España" ("Round-Trip to Spain"), as it is variously labeled, is a projected work revealing both the nostalgic reflections of a lonely expatriate, and the sorrowful disillusionment of an old man whose cherished dream of returning to his native land was tarnished by the unexpectedly painful reality of the experience. Among these notes are frequent lines like the following:

To be Spanish is no more than to be strictly loyal. If this loyalty is corrupted, or if it begins to disappear, a Spaniard is no longer a Spaniard; he has ceased to be one.

In direst poverty, Spain, since it has nothing else, exalts its air . . . its breezes, its fragrance of thyme.

Spain is already a little of eternity, a little foretaste of eternity. That is why chance happenings are unimportant.

Spain. Who knows Spain? Spain always deals you a different kind of blow.

A poet said to me, "This Madrid . . . is forever doing everything possible to give one one more reason to leave. . . ."

Considering Spanish tirades, a powerful Spaniard might say: "Can this haughtiness be tolerated?" The Spaniard can permit himself everything but money.

Everyone believes himself a part of the heroic in history.

Spain. So poor that even its almonds turned bitter.

Spain, even in new things, wants to be old.

The binder labeled simply "God" ("Dios") is perhaps the most replete of the packets Ramón has left behind. Surprisingly free of his "gregueristic" cleverness or humor, more in keeping with the tone of pathos which pervades his last published works, *Letters to the Swallows* or *Letters to Myself* and the trajectory seen in the binders on "Editors" and "Spain," cited above, the Ramón who writes these notes, carefully shielding them from the eyes of even his beloved Luisa,[4] is a different Ramón. It is a Ramón who, abandoned, poor, sick, and humbled, now thinks in terms of life and death and eternal values. With almost childlike trust and sincerity, Ramón, in these notes, turns to the God he now perceives as a source of shelter and security. For once he earnestly does *not* desire to be humorous, to entertain, or be witty, as he reviews his position and defends his trust and confidence in this supreme and very necessary Being in lines like the following:

The man of faith enjoys constant sunshine. Faith is sunshine.

God has made a splendor every minute.

If words do not bring us to God, we are undoubtedly misusing them.

To God, nothing is indifferent or imperceptible.

The world is nothing more than God's poetry.

All that is delicate is an echo of God. The flute . . . any music, is an echo of the beyond.

God is an immense poet, the creator of poets, who created all things for the purpose of poetic contemplation.

Nothing is easier than to write our prayers to God and then read them. One writes common love letters; why not stir oneself to write letters of divine love to the Creator?

God forgives sinners, but not hypocrites.

One should fear God but not be afraid of Him.

The hardest thing in the world is prayer. That is why it produces miracles.

The greatest thing about God, what makes Him unique, is His continuity.

To be in good standing with God. Not for good or ill, but for the indescribable sensation of standing well with God.

Omnipotence takes care of everything.

All of this material is available for study by scholars.[5] It presents, however, a double challenge, for not only are the handwritten notes frequently almost undecipherable, but often it is difficult to determine whether or not parts of this material have already been published. Determining this will require tracking down, cataloguing and cross-checking Ramón's thousands of articles in newspapers and magazines in Spain and in many countries of Latin America — a laborious and extensive task which may never be undertaken.

CHAPTER 7

Style: Ramón's Expressive System

I *The Metaphor*

IT is a curious fact that, despite the awesome number of works he published, Ramón Gómez de la Serna will be remembered more for his *style* than for his *content,* more for *how* he wrote, than for *what* he wrote, for it is, above all, in his stylistic innovations that he has left his personal and enduring mark on Spanish literature. The ingenious powers of perception which he cultivated from childhood prompted him to creative innovations in the use of imagery so as to multiply its possibilities for creative and original expression. He led the way in the vanguard's rediscovery of the metaphor, endowing it with greater evocative powers than had any Spanish writer since Góngora. Rossi affirms that "after Ramón, the metaphor becomes essential in literature,"[1] and Cernuda, examining the major influences on the Generation of '25 and later poets, acknowledges Ramón as their major precursor, saying: "It is in Gómez de la Serna that our lyric finds its most important antecedent for certain 'new' forms."[2]

Metaphor allowed Ramón unlimited freedom for the exercise of his prodigious imagination and he said of it, "Among all the figures of speech, metaphor is the most essential," explaining:

> The metaphor is, after all, the expressoin of relativity. Modern man is more oscillating than men of any other age and is therefore, more metaphoric. He must subject one thing to the light of another. He sees everything united, juxtaposed, associated.... Ideas will be true for a season, glosses will become boring, theses will come to seem foolish, but good metaphors will flower for ages.[3]

For Ramón, everything, real or unreal, conjured up metaphors. He believed that "the image of just one thing now scarcely says anything. It is necessary to complicate it, to inject one within

[126]

Style: Ramón's Expressive System

another, to wound it"[4] and accordingly, he varied the construction of his images in a surprising number of ways. Frequently he used two or more consecutive images as, for example, when he says, "María Mallo appears [1] like a truly new springtime in the air of Madrid, [2] like a gift of May. . . ."[5]

When no precise word or adjective was available to express the comparisons which suggested themselves to his fancy, he coined adjectives of whole phrases like the following: "Packages like women's torsos in corsets,"[6] or "Weak and wheezing as if after a pneumonia of both lungs and the soul."[7] Frequently he brought into play the parts or properties of elements comprising his basic metaphors. He described Spain, for example, as "a brain in which all the regions are a circumlocution, a lobule, a phrenological number, each and all necessary to the nature of the whole."[8]

One of his favorite devices was to effect comparisons between expressed or implied properties of basic metaphors which he allowed to remain unexpressed, apparently expecting the reader to intuit them. For example, when he writes that Neruda's verse, "begins soft, but in the curve of its thigh one feels the push given it by curve and protrusion,"[9] he implicitly equates the body of verse with the human body. Frequently he implies rather than expresses the elements of his comparison, alluding implicitly, for example, to Goya's paintings when he says that Goya is "that multiple mirror before which one shaves off foolishness."[10]

Sometimes, he presents parallel chains of both expressed and implicit images to create unusual and impressionistic descriptions, as when he writes: "In the garden was a well, and in it, the hours of the Golden Age fell and drowned."[11] Here he has established a series of partially expressed and partially implied equations: Golden Age = autumn; years = trees; hours = leaves. Apparently, he either envisioned this whole sequence with extremely rapid perception or intuited it in one instantaneous "vision." Varying his use of these implicit, or subconsciously associated elements in images, Ramón sometimes suppressed or compressed them in such a way as to convert whole phrases into simple appositives, as for example, when he wrote, "He possessed the sword of conversation,"[12] implying the unexpressed image "swordlike dexterity of conversation."

Ramón Gómez de la Serna utilized verbs in a similar manner, choosing those so rich in associations that they imply or act as images, as for example, when he says, "Velázquez *tutea* el tiempo," roughly equivalent to "Velázquez is chummy with time and space."[13] Sometimes his preoccupation with creating unusual images led him to attribute unreal or impossible qualities to his subjects, as when he says of Azorín, "He walks a little on tiptoe . . . hands tranquilly placed in the pockets of his soul."[14] Surrealistic images, effecting a comparison between real elements and others based upon reality, yet exceeding it, may also be found in Ramón's works, as when he writes, "The clocks, with their two round wounds were bleeding time. . . ."[15] Certain conceptual associations recur frequently enough to indicate that Ramón had a predilection for them. The three most discernible are: (1) visual, name-associated images; (2) animal images; and (3) religious images. The written, visual form of letters or names frequently suggested to him images like the following:

"KFK," standing, its F held by two K's like bookends. . . .[16]

"T" is the hammer of the alphabet. . . .[17]

"B" is the nursemaid of the alphabet. . . .[18]

Animal images, perhaps attributable in part to the essential childlikeness of Ramón's nature, are also abundant in his works. Curiously, among all the critics who have discussed his use of imagery or his *greguerías,* only Murciano has commented upon the frequent recurrence of animal images.[19] Usually, they seem to have been suggested either by something in his subjects's work (as the bird images in Poe, and the cat images in Colette), or by some aspect of his subjects' physical appearance. Ramón tells us, for example, that Kafka had "large ears like a white bat";[20] Unamuno had "a face like a young owl,"[21] and Cansinos' face seemed like that of a "mystical horse."[22] The small, slightly deformed, black-clad figure of María Blanchard, caused Ramón to refer to her as "a little black spider."[23] On occasion, Ramón described his own feelings by using animal images, as when he said, "I felt like a winter bat who wanted to pass for a swallow."[24] His metaphoric menagerie also comprised roosters, rats, cats, dogs, tigers, lions, bears, onagers, serpents, horses, deer, fish, and even legendary animals such as marine monsters, satyrs, and dragons.[25]

Religious imagery appears frequently in Ramón's works. This imagery might be expected of a writer from a country with such strong religious traditions as Spain. Given, moreover, Ramón's propensity to consider artist-creators as elect, often martyr-like individuals, the abundance of such imagery in his biographical works seems a natural

Style: Ramón's Expressive System

development. Hornedo, a Spanish Jesuit, seems to be the only critic who has noted the abundance of religious images in Ramón's works. He comments that:

> Gómez de la Serna shows . . . a singular predilection for images and comparisons taken from liturgy, from ecclesiastical persons and customs, and even from the mysteries and sacraments of Catholicism.[26]

Hornedo cites examples from *Pombo,* the *Greguerías,* and *Contemporary Portraits* to substantiate his claim, and contends that the persistence of such images in Ramón's works is a manifestation of the latent faith which contributed to his eventual return to the religious beliefs and practices in which he had been reared. Some examples are:

> The period of Cubism was nothing more than a period of penance, of temporary vows in the cloister of reason.[27]

> As it was raining we went beneath umbrellas, like bishops under canopies.[28]

> His kindly look, which lifts all excommunications.[29]

> There are some days, blue or grey, but with the coldness of the Final Judgment.[30]

> He endures a heavy asceticism . . . he has a firm redemption to accomplish.[31]

II Other Figurative Devices

A. *Personification and Hyperbole* As might be expected in a writer as charmed by *things* as was Ramón, nonrational entities are frequently endowed with human qualities in his writing. Del Río says that in Ramón, "beings and things seem mixed, without a dividing line; the human becomes just one more mechanism; and the inert shows itself to us with attributes of the living."[32] Examples like the following are frequent:

> The shop windows of Madrid . . . looked at him astonished. . . .[33]

> Opulent matrons — magazines — are charitable enough to give emergency nursing to the hungry poor, a few saving drops from their opulent breasts.[34]

Picasso flees and hides . . . so much, that sometimes the hotel where he is living changes streets and not only is he not to be found in it . . . but the hotel itself is not to be found. In its place stands only an empty lot, whistling, pretending to be unconcerned.[35]

Ramón also had a propensity for hyperbole, which he used sometimes for its deforming, caricaturesque value, sometimes for stress or emphasis and sometimes, purely on humorous impulse. Salaverría says, "Verbal inebriation carried him to disturbing exaggerations and hyperboles."[36] Some instances of Ramón's varying uses of hyperbole follow:

Don Ramón on grey days in his country home, would get into bed and eventually came to forget how to walk.[37]

[Referring to Unamuno's visits to Madrid] He prepared for that arrival as for the sailing of a marine squadron, during the Spanish-American War.[38]

[Referring to Oscar Wilde] He always wore his lovely tie-pin . . . he would have stuck it into the skin of his chest if he had had to go naked.[39]

B. *The Greguería* The expressive or figurative device for which Ramón is best known is that of his own invention — the *greguería*. How he invented it pertains to his life story. Here, only its essence and use will be considered. When Ramón invented this expressive device in 1910, the word *greguería* (as we have seen earlier), occurred to him as a possible name for it. Although the word's dictionary definition did not really describe the mode of expression he had invented, he used it, nevertheless, "because of its euphony."[40] Etymologically, according to Corominas, the word *greguería* derives from *gringo* "in the sense of an incomprehensible language," and was first listed officially in the *Diccionario de Autoridades* in 1734, where it was defined as meaning *algarabía,* in reference to the incomprehensible Arabic language.[41] When Gómez de la Serna comments upon the meaning of the word, he says:

Greguería, algarabía, outcry, confused outcry. . . . That which things shout out. At least, there is no doubt that I have baptized my genre with a word that was lost in the dictionary, that wasn't the name of anything, and which now, when pronounced . . . refers to me, who changed its meaning, who converted it into something it was not.[42]

The *greguería* became for him a manner of expression, which he both described and defined, saying:

Style: Ramón's Expressive System

The *greguería* is the attempt to define that which cannot be defined, to capture the fleeting. . . .[43]

Greguerías are merely fatal exclamations of things and of the soul, upon bumping into one another by pure chance.[44]

Humor + metaphor = *greguería*.[45]

The *greguería* is all that Ramón has claimed, and more. It is "the art of the subtle sensation,"[46] the ability to "sidetrack with humor"[47] the ordinary meanings of words and concepts in order to express the inexpressible. It is a glimpse — generally a humorous and audacious glimpse — of the unsuspected, the unencounterable, the ephemeral and yet, somehow, it always has its roots in reality. Ramón has carefully distinguished his *greguerías* from reflections, paradoxes, maxims, adages, proverbs, refrains, aphorisms, exclamations, and just plain nonsense. He has affirmed that the true *greguería* must not be merely a descriptive phrase nor a platitude; it must not be too sentimental nor too short. The *greguería*, according to its creator, may utilize any of the other figures of speech, such as metaphor, simile, hyperbaton, hyperbole, synecdoche, metonymy, or anaphora. It may use homonyms, paranyms, puns, and even *jitanjáforas* or nonsense words. Because it embraces every aspect of life and every sort of trope, Ramón has aptly called the *greguería* "*the amoeba of the new.*"[48]

Ramón found antecedents for his *greguerías* in the short Japanese *haiku* poems and in the romantic Arabic-Andaluz poetic *kasidas,* both of which are rich in imagery. Ramón did not pretend to have written the first *greguerías,* but he did believe he was the first to become conscious of them as a new kind of entity or genre, and to cultivate them deliberately. Occasional *greguerías* may be found in the works of writers from the classic to the contemporary period, and Ramón cited examples of *greguerías* he had garnered from widely varied sources, from classical writers such as Lucian, Horace and Ovid, to modern and contemporary writers such as Zorilla, Chekhov, Cocteau, Baudelaire, Rimbaud, Breton, Wilde, Darío, and Lorca.[49]

Some writers, like Cansinos Asséns, seem to overlook the essentially metaphoric nature of the *greguerías* when they contend (probably because of their brevity and humor) that the *doloras* or *humoradas* of Campoamor may be considered forerunners of the *greguerías*.[50] Cansinos Asséns also errs in his insistence that the *greguerías* are essentially caricatures, for while caricaturesque elements may frequently be found in them, it is not one of their essential components. When Ramón says, for example, "A concert program ... the music menu,"[51] he has turned out a perfect *greguería* but no element of caricature is involved. Apart from the use of imagery, the *greguerías* do not have any single essential component. Nevertheless, they do have some identifiable characteristics. Salinas, for example, claims that instantaneousness and condensation mark the *greguería* and explains: "The *greguería* ought to be a sudden, brief revelation which, by virtue of its unusual manner of relating ideas or things, lights up for us a new vision of something."[52] Tomás Borrás claims somewhat exaggeratedly that *greguerías* are not metaphors, but discoveries.[53] Gaspar Gómez de la Serna comes closer to the truth than most critics when he affirms that the *greguerías* are:

> Sudden and metaphoric insights into the meanings of things which concern planes of reality hidden to logical thinking through recourse to intuitive and subconscious sources. . . .
> It is a genre of prose which . . . does not obey the characteristics of deductive thought, but of feeling or living thought. . . .[54]

Cernuda stresses their peculiarly poetic nature when he affirms that:

> The *greguería* arrives at poetry by an indirect route: by a play of wit . . . it is at times a minute prose poem. . . . This relates Gómez de la Serna with our culturalist and conceptist prose and poetry; which also are connected with the young poets of 1925.[55]

Careful study of Ramón's *greguerías* reveals that they possess four consistent characteristics: (1) they are always based upon images (which are generally metaphors); (2) they are brief; (3) they are self-sufficient (that is, they do not rely on surrounding context for their meaning or effect); (4) they contain an element of surprise which frequently is humorously expressed.

In the following *greguerías,* all of these characteristics are revealed. These examples also indicate the great variety of tropes and literary devices which Ramón used in composing his *greguerías:*

(1) *Greguerías* using simile or metaphor: She laughed and shook hands as if she were tolling the bell of friendship.[56]

Wilde had the sponge of his brain sopped with tedium.[57]

Style: Ramón's Expressive System

(2) *Greguerías* combining hyperbole and personification:

He recited his verse in all the principal salons, and hearing him, the sofas fainted, turning into divans.[58]

When a nation is at war, its fountains weep instead of pouring out plain water.[59]

(3) *Greguerías* using paronomasia:

The *glosser* seems like a *glutton* who tastes everything....[60]

(4) *Greguerías* based upon visual images:

Madame Stäel — with two lovely beauty marks in her name....[61]

His moustache is the black border on the sympathy card of his face.[62]

(5) *Greguerías* using caricature:

[Describing Queen María Luisa] A woman who would elbow anyone she wished to greet, should he pass by, distracted; her fans were her best weapon.[63]

(6) There is another type of *greguería* which might be labeled the "capsule synthesis" or "flash of insight" *greguería*. García-Luengo seems to have perceived it dimly when he said that the *greguería* "at times surprises with rapid synthesis and unsuspected associations which may seem arbitrary, but which have a lightning-like effect, illuminating zones of reality for us."[64]

These *greguerías* provide capsule syntheses or flashes of luminous insight into the subject, life, or work to which they refer. In the biographies they serve as instances of witty, pointed, and valorative synthesis. They may refer to the subject's work — Goya's art is described, for example, as "tremulous bites of the truth of life,"[65] and as "that multimirror in which to shave off frustrations."[66] More often, however, they refer to the individuals who are the subjects of the biographies. Examples of some of Ramón's most concise and expressive "capsule" descriptions follow:

Velázquez Uses familiar address with time and space.[67]

Juan Ramón Jiménez Juan Ramón is the farewell scenery takes of scenery.[68]

Baudelaire	Holds a pain pill close in his mouth.[69]
Benavente	In everything he's like that. . . . very Duke of Alba in miniature.[70]
Répide	He was a character out of Ramón de la Cruz, painted by Goya.[71]
Charles Chaplin	Chaplin is the seriousness that gravely mocks at laughter behind its back.[72]
Quevedo	He *is* the off-the-cuff remark.[73]
Nerval	He felt . . . somewhat like life's bastard's child.[74]
Silverio Lanza	. . . is a man who would address a prostitute formally.[75]
Valle-Inclán	The best masked figure that ever crossed Alcalá Street afoot.[76]
Azorín	He *is* the preterit perfect.[77]

As for the importance of the *greguería* in Ramón's expressive system, he readily admitted that he did not write constantly in *greguerías,* saying:

> My harvest of *greguerías* is not constant. It blossoms only occasionally — very occasionally. . . . They do not come in quantity. They can never be sought out. One must wait for them.[78]

He tells us that, like a patient fisherman, he would "spend days and days waiting for those that are *[greguerías]* are repeatedly tossing back into the water those that are only sardines,"[79] and he reiterates this often, insisting: "The *greguería* is not an easy genre."[80]

From his own words as well as from careful observation of his work, it would seem then that those who contend that the *greguería* is the basic element of Gómez de la Serna's style have allowed themselves to be dazzled by the frequency of its appearance into believing that it is everpresent in his writing. It is not the *greguería,* but the *image* that is everpresent. It exists both in the *greguerías* and in their absence. His images do not "jell" into self-sufficient

Style: Ramón's Expressive System [135]

greguerías each time he expresses an unexpected comparison, or plays with words. It is the image, rather than the *greguería* which is the basic element of his style, and the image he uses most frequently is the metaphor. It is precisely for this reason that Gómez de la Serna has enlivened, varied, and multiplied the image's potential in every way possible.

Nevertheless, critics like Rafael Calleja are justified when they speak of Ramón's desire to "greguerize everything" and describe the *greguería* as infiltrating all of Ramón's works in every genre,[81] for, as Cardona has stated, "The linguistic and psychic factors which take place in the formation of such tropes are without doubt the same that take place in the formation of the *greguería*.[82] Guillermo de Torre, while agreeing that Ramón's works are not merely extended *greguerías* as some critics claim, adds, "They are not *greguerías* properly speaking, but the greater part of his work is indeed dominated by a gregueristic spirit."[83]

III *Structural Devices*

Since Gómez de la Serna was essentially a creator, he sought new modes of expression not only through imagery, but through language itself, playing with words and conceptual structures as ingeniously as he played with metaphors and other tropes to achieve new meanings and effects. Because words are the units from which expressive structures are built, Ramón refused to see them as static entities. His attitude toward words is expressed in an essay he entitled "Words and the Inexpressible" ("Las palabras y lo indecible") where he writes:

> The new poetry and new literature have liberated words, and words act on their own account, following an unconcious and sure law. . . .
> Let us enter into the inexpressible like discoverers, finding new materials. . . .[84]

To this end, he invented various ways of applying new meanings and powers to words. The success of his efforts caused Yndurain to say "Ramón is the first in Spain who has seen the magic capacity of the word and has explored the ample gambit of its possibilities. . . ."[85] Senabre insisted that Ramón's wordplay in the *greguerías* "is not a matter of simple wordplay, but of a type of construction which translates into language a specific attitude of the author."[86]

Ramón's attitude toward language was essentially that of a

creator. He, obviously, was determined to master words and to use them to mean just what he chose. He both ascribed meanings to words and words to meanings. Senabre, noting Ramón's proclivity toward false etymology in his wordplay, attributes it to his essentially childlike and innovative vision, explaining that:

> Ramón, at times, places himself before words as before a new and marvelous reality ... adopting the new and uncontaminated gaze of a child.... It is an ingenious attitude which immediately establishes a logical relation between the meaning of a word and the concept he assigns it. A clash results because the correspondence does not really exist....[87]

This type of word play may be seen in instances like the following:

> El Greco understood *velvet,* the only *skin* created by man[88] (a play on the words *pelo* and *piel* from *terciopelo,* velvet, and *piel,* skin).

> He is *gallant* ... for he *regales* poetry ... and it is for this reason, for *regaling gifts* that a *gallant* is called *gallant.*[89] (There is a play on the words *galas,* gifts; *regalar,* to give gifts; and *gala,* festive.)

Senabre also notes Ramón's use of "paronomasia," a play on cognates derived from the same root having phonetic but not necessarily semantic or conceptual similarity. In this type of word play meaning is secondary, and Senabre, studying its use in the *greguerías,* believes that Ramón used it chiefly for acoustic effect. His opinion seems to be borne out in the following examples:

> ... *season* after *season* that theater presented his works to a *seasoned* public...[90]

> *Chagall* ... is the *jackal* of modern painting.[91]

Frequently, Gómez de la Serna created words either by adding suffixes where they were not usually applied, or by combining several words into one, conveying a mental association which had occurred to him. The following examples show suffix-formed neologisms:

> We are ... streeters and nocturnophiles.[92]

> This slowifying of any scene...[93]

> Poor and carpentery....[94]

Style: Ramón's Expressive System

The main altars . . . encandling themselves with candles.[95]

His emigrantic soul . . .[96]

It wasn't an agony . . . it was an agonosity.[97]

Streetwalking and overnightery writer.[98]

The neologisms he formed by combining two apparently unrelated words may be seen in these examples:

Multitasting life. . . .[99]

In his drunkenness there is an alchodrama.[100]

Maruja confronts the vitadimensional. . . .[101]

In addition to experimenting with the meanings, associations, and formations of words, Ramón also experimented with relationships and juxtapositions of concepts and ideas.

Almost as an extension of his use of imagery, he often employed analogy, writing for example:

Like the pianist he is, he writes as if playing the piano.[102]

Just as Goya converted his appetite into color . . . he converted it into musical notes.[103]

Frequently Ramón juxtaposed paradoxical concepts to express apparently contradictory, unbelievable, or absurd statements that were actually true in fact, or simply when he wanted to combine two apparently opposed ideas to express a truth. Often he established the point of contact between opposing concepts through the sheer force of his ingenuity, as, for example, when he wrote:

Nothing has remained so unwritten as that prose. . . . [104]

One sees him passing through the sadness of life, enjoying himself.[105]

His soul is a web, a clear web, but after all a web.[106]

Ramón seemed to enjoy playing with antithetical constructions for he not only juxtaposed antithetical elements, he frequently did so in pairs or multiple sets. In such cases they usually do not carry his ideas forward, but merely reaffirm, restate, or reinforce them. Generally, he first advances a positive concept, then negates or opposes it as in the following examples:

> Unamuno has always been provoking and denying his provocations, advancing and receding. . . . [107]

> All his work is that: the idea and its contradiction, faith and skepticism.[108]

> . . . He wants to swindle the concrete, returning it to its inconcreteness, moved by the innate desire to hand over the discovered to the will of indiscovery.[109]

Frequently too, Ramón employed negative structures reminiscent of the "not A but B" constructions found so often in Góngora's poetry; as for example:

> His enormous forehead is not the dome but the pantheon of the idea.[110]

Frequently Ramón expands such structures providing a "Not A or B but C" pattern, as when he says:

> Quevedo passed through life leaving a path not at all academic, not at all awarded, but true.[111]

Another variation is the not "A, but B, C, and D" pattern:

> Benedetta's art is no longer a contemplation, but a direction, an arrow . . . a labyrinth.[112]

Perhaps one of the most delightful techniques Ramón employed in his conceptual play is that which might be labeled "disruption of normal thought sequences." This hitherto disregarded rhetorical device studied by Carlos Bousoño in *Teoría de la expresión poética,* is a technique causing humorous effects by disrupting logical sequences or relationships which experience or intuition have conditioned the reader to expect.[113] Its effectiveness becomes readily apparent in the examples below:

> He had curly, unshorn hair, in which his ideas got matted.[114]

> Lope is going to become a priest. He goes to Toledo to this end, and the bishop accepts him, but makes him cut off his moustache.[115]

Style: Ramón's Expressive System

Sometimes, pondering seriously what might have become of Valle-Inclán's arm, I have seen it changed into a gargoyle, one of those gargoyles on our cathedrals.[116]

In Ramón, rather than the result of mere verbosity, as some critics have maintained, proliferation seems to be a manifestation of his unhurried manner of expression and deliberate striving for tone and effect. He used pleonasms (repetition of words or ideas) for acoustic, alliterative effects, often coining words to achieve the desired repetive effect, as in the following examples:

He is a labyrinth of a man, worth entering in order to become enlabyrinthed.[117]

Completely complete, Velázquez never stumbles. . . .[118]

He was a traveling newsman, a supposer of novel suppositions. . . .[119]

Cansinos chatted to chat, spoke to speak in the dawn.[120]

Sometimes Ramón seemed to take delight in enumeration for its own sake, but frequently his enumerative passages achieve a certain rhythmic effect through the use of deliberate reiterations of words, syllables, and phonemes, as for example, when he writes:

. . . he lives in a house with good curtains and good furniture . . . has good positions . . . and Big Bank Bills (Buenos Billetes de Banco).[121]

One of Ramón's favorite techniques is to wander off from the main path of his prose in order to explore numerous conceptual variations before continuing. Dámaso Alonso, who has studied the use of such tactics in *Seis calas en el estudio de la expresión literaria,* developed a pattern system to aid in the study of such structures, labeling nonprogressive variations $A_1, A_2, A_3, \ldots A_n$, as an indication that they retain the same syntactic function, and do not advance the concept but are only conceptual variations. Progressive units he labeled progressively, A, B, C, and so forth.

Sample passages by Ramón, written in similar subordinations below, for purposes of analysis, make this kind of nonprogressive play quite evident:

His art (A)
    delicate (a_1),
    poetic (a_2),
    ornate (a_3), needed (B) much accord (C_1),
                            much intonation (C_2),
                              much illusion (C_3).[122]

And it is that Azorín (A) is (B) sufficiently friendly
                                with himself (C_1),
                 sufficiently decent
                                with himself (C_2),
                 sufficiently in accord
                              with himself (C_3),

to maintain (D) that density (E)
                personal (e_1),
                intransferable (e_2),
                possessed (e_3),
                heavy. . . . (e_4),
    with a weight (F) that is
                undeclinable and (f_1),
                touching (f_2).[123]

Because of such exuberant repetitions, ornamentations and proliferations, some critics, like Salaverría, have labeled Ramón a "baroque" writer.[124] The term is an appropriate one. Ramón's use of proliferative phrases is not accidental. The examples below have been arranged so as to stress the deliberate plurifications they evince and to indicate when and how they occur. Often they seem contrived either to achieve effects of crescendo and decrescendo, or to present variations on a theme. The following demonstrates their use in crescendo and decrescendo effects:

    The city . . . was experiencing a novel attack,
                          a delirium of suppositions,
                          an orgy of verifications.[125]

    . . . he throws himself into it in consolation
                              of his thirst,
                              of his anger,
                              of his creative
                                    desperation[126]

Style: Ramón's Expressive System

> It frightens me . . . seeing his evolution toward the
>   implacable
> and seeing how he kills the artist
>   in himself, through
>   his anguishes,
>   his fears,
>   his cares, and
>   his piddly missions.[127]

Ramón also adorned simple concepts with a variety of purely ornamental variations, as for example:

> Nerval . . . writes . . . letters and more letters,
>   full of sighs,
>   bordered with sighs,
>   handwritten with sighs.[128]

Critics, even admiring critics, who have commented on the proliferative qualities of Ramón's style, have often done him a disservice by dismissing it as mere verbosity. Torrente Ballester, for example, wrote:

> Ramón lacks a sense of norm and limit; his capacity for writing can only be compared to his capacity for speaking . . . This superabundance determines the baroque character of his style, whose richness of vocabulary and syntactic formulas have no contemporary counterpart and only admit similarity . . . with Quevedo's prose.[129]

Chabás said, somewhat disparagingly, "One might say that this writer, having acquired the habit of his very original contortions, imitates himself."[130]

Their tone, like that of most critics on this point, falls halfway between praise and blame. It is as if they do not approve of such proliferations, but are afraid to condemn them entirely, lest buried beneath the verbiage there might perhaps lie an as yet undiscovered treasure. Salaverría perhaps achieves the neatest balance between praise and condemnation when he comments that Ramón does not presume to purity of style, but reaches out beyond grammar so that he dominates language. He adds:

Seldom has such an example of inebriation, delirium, enthusiasm, verbal furor, been seen. With phrases, and clauses, he does in the XX century what Quevedo did in the XVII.
Gómez de la Serna's language is begging for a name: baroquism. . . . Words pile up, turn, return, converge, disintegrate, form curves and rare designs; among these multiple, multiple-ending words are ideas, tremulous ideas.[131]

It is an injustice to Ramón that his literary genius has too often been dismissed with the superficial evaluation of words like "ingenious" and "baroque," for careful study reveals that his multiple forms of word play, structural juxtapositions, and proliferation are deliberate rhetorical devices designed to achieve specific effects and ends. Ramón is indeed a truly creative literary artist.

IV *Re-creative Techniques in Biographical Writing*

Stylistically it should be noted that in his biographical writing, Gómez de la Serna strove not merely to narrate his subjects' lives, but also, as nearly as possible, to conjure up their presence. He did this principally in three ways: (1) through a novel use of description; (2) through imitation of characteristic elements of their literary styles; (3) through a liberal use of anecdote.

Ramón seemed incapable of writing objective description. Instead, he employed images to describe almost every aspect of his subjects. As a descriptive technique, imagery offered him unlimited advantages over objective description, enabling him to suggest far more than he stated, and to infer the personal, moral, mental, or spiritual qualities he perceived in his subjects. Facial features, facial expressions, clothing, the subject's manner of walking, airs, and manners as Ramón presented them, all reveal a great deal about his subjects. Frequently he produces the tone, style, and dominant characteristics of his subject's own writing. It is an effective device, cleverly insinuating his subject's actual presence into his biography. Azorín, for example, has a slow-paced, enumerative, and repetitive style which Ramón skillfully reproduced. When writing of Valle-Inclán, he utilized a grotesque type of description highly reminiscent of those used in Valle's *esperpentos*. Treating Quevedo, he was deliberately baroque and somewhat *tremendista*. In *Kafka,* he not only managed to create precisely the tone and spirit he identified with Kafka and his work, a labyrinthine, surrealistic tone of paradox, loneliness, and despair; he also imitated Kafka'a use of religious symbolism.

Style: Ramón's Expressive System

He interwove real and fictional events when writing of Pirandello, and since Rémy de Gourmont was a symbolist, when writing of him, Ramón began his biography with a five-page digressive "parenthesis of symbolism"[132] in which he presented his subject wholly through symbols, showing Gourmont as a bishop in the cathedral of style. The stones of the cathedral represented filigrees of his style, the panes of the stained glass windows, his words; his stories were described as having a confessional flavor, his prose as the oil maintaining the flame of the sanctuary light, and so on.

When treating of poets, Ramón wrote, as one might expect, more poetically than ever. Thus, for example, in writing of Baudelaire he uses musical effects as well as abundant imagery. He writes lyrically of Juan Ramón Jiménez, and when writing of Poe, imitates him effectively by employing morbidly dramatic images and repeated alliterations. When presenting dynamic, colorful personalities like Valle-Inclán, Quevedo, Wilde or Shaw, Ramón seemed to feel that such figures were best shown in action. Consequently, although anecdote appears in all his biographies, it predominates in these. The anecdotes Ramón relates may or may not be true. As a creative artist, he freely created or invented anecdotes illustrating the sort of thing that *might* have happened to his subjects, and which served to reveal their traits of character in a more aesthetic or dynamic manner than a mere mention of them might have achieved.

In Valle-Inclán, for example, Ramón utilizes whole chains of anecdotes, some absurd, some exaggerated, some grotesque, and many untrue, but all conveying the obstreperousness of his character. Through anecdote we see Valle disrupting the first-night performances of Echegaray's plays, defying police and city officials, quarreling with Unamuno, pawning his belongings, and generally outraging friends and enemies alike. Stories telling how he had lost his arm abounded. Ramón collected twelve such tales and added his own invented anecdotes to them. He tells us, for example, that Valle's arm was variously eaten by a lion, stolen as a relic, severed by a rival, and/or pawned when he needed money. Ramón even advanced the theory that a mysterious equation existed between Valle's flowing beard and missing arm, so that were the beard to be suddenly clipped, the arm would grow back.

In *Quevedo* Ramón again utilized anecdote to illustrate his subject's irascibility and shows him attacking and being attacked in turn by Lope, Góngora, and Calderón. He re-creates the flamboyant, dandified and self-assured figure of Oscar Wilde principally through anecdote, and allows Wilde's outrageous impudence to reveal itself by describing incidents like the one in which he appeared before the audience after the first performance of *The Importance of Being Ernest,* congratulated them for having had the good fortune to see it, and gave them his evaluation of the work: "The first act is ingenious, the second, marvelous, and the third, abominably masterful."[133] Later, when Wilde's life and career had been totally destroyed by his public condemnation and prison term, Ramón again had recourse to anecdote — both real and invented — to depict his complete degeneration. He portrayed Wilde as dependent upon the charity of his hotel-keeper for a place to stay, begging money from former friends, and attempting excruciatingly to resume his writing. He invented anecdotes to emphasize Wilde's tragic abandonment, depicting his solitary walks by the sea, the mesmerizing effect of the waves upon his consciousness, and his temptations to suicide.

Ramón's use of anecdote served an aesthetic purpose: it highlighted aspects of his subjects' personalities and aided in their re-creation by achieving greater vitality than would have been possible through simple narration or more traditional and less imaginative study. By relying almost as heavily upon anecdote as upon narration, and by using imagery and imitation to open new perspectives of artistic expression and biographic re-creation, Gómez de la Serna brought his creative subjective approach even to the writing of biography; it "Ramonized" them and made them artistic and poetic creations.

CHAPTER 8

Conclusion

RAMÓN Gómez de la Serna was a dedicated literary creator who essayed every genre but poetry, and essayed even that indirectly. Despite the incredible variety in his works, the myriad plot ideas in his novelistic writing, and the boundless interests manifested in his essays, however, Ramón's writing always retained a curious sameness. All his works abound in imagery, vitality, and free poetic expression. All display innovation, experimentation, and whimsical ingenuity. Classifications and genres overlap in his writing. Creativity, originality, and humor stand out.

Gómez de la Serna was not a scholar, not a researcher, not a deep seeker of eternal truths. To judge him in such terms would be to evaluate the beauty and merit of a hummingbird by the criterion designed for a hawk. Like the hummingbird, Ramón belongs in the light category. It is *how* rather than *what*, *style* rather than *content*, which are essential in Ramón and which have had a significant influence upon subsequent Spanish literature. Ramón utilized just about every variety of rhetorical image to surpass reality and to present that marginally conscious zone which lies beyond our commonplace concepts of the "real." Because his creative innovations succeeded in expanding the expressive powers of the image, he has been recognized as a major influence on the Spanish poets of the Generation of '25 and one of the major precursors of the "new" Spanish literature.[1]

Simultaneously impressionistic and expressionistic, Ramón rarely described anything objectively, but rather in terms of how it seemed to him, and how it made him feel. In all that he wrote, he expressed himself; his subjects, both fictional and biographical, are projections of his own life and personality. A true vanguardist, a creative genius ahead of his time, Ramón has yet to receive the full recognition he so well deserves. Too long has he been considered merely a clever verbal gymnast, a literary magician, or even a clown among writers. Now perhaps, as a more sophisticated public seeks and appreciates artistic variety and innovation, the time may finally have come for a new evaluation of the literary worth of Ramón Gómez de la Serna and his works.

Notes and References

Chapter One

1. Ramón Gómez de la Serna, *Automoribundia* (Buenos Aires: Editorial Sudamericana, 1948), p. 61. Hereafter referred to as *Auto.*
2. *Ibid.,* p. 77.
3. Ramón Gómez de la Serna, *Total de greguerías* (Madrid: Aguilar, 1955), p. 438.
4. *Ibid.,* p. 469.
5. Gaspar Gómez de la Serna, *Ramón* (Madrid: Taurus Ediciones, 1963), p. 116.
6. Ramón Gómez de la Serna, "Gravedad e importancia del humorismo," *Revista de Occidente,* XXVIII (1930), 351.
7. Robert Shattuck, *The Banquet Years* (New York: Doubleday and Co., 1961), pp. 28-29.
8. *Auto.,* p. 810.
9. *Ibid.,* pp. 214-22.
10. *Ibid.,* p. 281.
11. *Ibid.,* p. 250.
12. Ramón Gómez de la Serna, *Total de greguerías,* p. xxiii.
13. *Auto.,* pp. 210-12.
14. Gaspar Gómez de la Serna, *Ramón,* p. 73.
15. Rodolfo Cardona, *Ramón, A Study of Gómez de la Serna and His Works* (New York: Eliseo Torres and Sons, 1957), p. 34.
16. Ramón Gómez de la Serna, *Azorín* (Buenos Aires: Editorial Losada, 1942), prologue, p. 7.
17. Ramón Gómez de la Serna, *Biografías completas* (Madrid: Aguilar, 1959), p. 1374. Hereafter referred to as *B.C.*
18. Rodolfo Cardona, "Ramón Gómez de la Serna," *Novelistas españoles de hoy* (New York: W.W. Norton, 1959), p. 16.
19. Ramón Gómez de la Serna, *Don Ramón María del Valle-Inclán* (Buenos Aires: Espasa-Calpe Argentina, 1944), p. 41. Hereafter referred to as *V.I.*
20. Julián Marías, "Ramón y la realidad," *Insula* (Madrid), XII (February 15, 1957), 2, 8.

21. Robert J. Loy, "Things in Recent French Literature," *PMLA*, LXXI (March, 1956), 28-29.
22. Julián Marías, personal interview with the present author, Indiana University, October 25, 1967.
23. Cardona, *Ramón*, p. 38.
24. Federico Carlos Sainz de Robles, "Ramón: Antena, Inmunidad, Influencia," *Revista de Ideas Estéticas* (Madrid), XXI (1963), 6-7.
25. Julián Marías, "El final de la *Automoribundia*," in *El tiempo que ni vuelve ni tropieza* (Barcelona and Buenos Aires: Editora y Distribuidora Hispano Americana, 1964), p. 213.
26. José Ortega y Gasset, *The Dehumanization of Art*, trans. by William R. Trask (New York: Doubleday, 1956), pp. 33-38.
27. Ramón Gómez de la Serna, *Ramonismo* (Madrid: Calpe, 1923), p. 5.
28. *Ibid.*, p. 18.
29. *Ibid.*, pp. 241-43.
30. Ramón Gómez de la Serna, *El incongruente* (Madrid: Calpe, 1922), p. 14.
31. Cardona, *Ramón*, p. 22.
32. Guillaume Apollinaire, *Il y a . . . Poesies et prose inédites*. Preface by Ramón Gómez de la Serna (Paris: Albert Messein, 1925), n.p.
33. Gaspar Gómez de la Serna, *Ramón*, p. 160.
34. José Pla, "Ramón Gómez de la Serna," *Grandes Tipos* (Barcelona: Editorial Aedos, 1959), p. 33.
35. Ramón Gómez de la Serna, *Los muertos, las muertas, y otras fantasmagorías* (Madrid: Cruz y raya, 1935). p. 17.
36. *Auto.*, p. 609.
37. Pedro Massa, personal interview, Instituto cultural de España, Buenos Aires, December 21, 1972.
38. Antonio Valencia, "El otro Ramón de América," *Arriba* (Madrid, January 15, 1963), pp. 2-3.
39. Ramón Gómez de la Serna, *Nostalgias de Madrid* (Madrid: Editorial El Grifón de Plata, 1956), pp. 16-19.
40. Gaspar Gómez de la Serna, *Ramón*, p. 249.
41. *Ibid.*, p. 251.
42. *Ibid.*, p. 254.
43. *Ibid.*, p. 255.
44. *Ibid.*, p. 257.
45. *Ibid.*, p. 261.

Chapter Two

1. Ramón Gómez de la Serna, *Automoribundia* (Buenos Aires: Editorial Sudamericana, 1948), p. 206.
2. *Ibid.*, p. 506.
3. *Ibid.*, p. 206.

4. Ramón Gómez de la Serna, *Obras completas, I* (Barcelona: Editorial AHR, 1956), p. 357.

Chapter Three

1. Ramón Gómez de la Serna, *La nardo* (Madrid: Editorial Ulises, 1930), p. 123. Hereafter referred to as *Nardo*.
2. Ramón Gómez de la Serna, *La mujer de ámbar* (Buenos Aires: Espasa-Calpe Argentina, Colección Austral, 1948), prologue, p. 7.
3. Rodolfo Cardona, *Ramón, A Study of Gómez de la Serna and His Works* (New York: Eliseo Torres and Sons, 1957), p. 56.
4. Ramón Gómez de la Serna, *El torero Caracho* (Paris, Madrid, & Lisbon: Editorial Agencia Mundial de Librería, 1926), pp. 228-30.
5. *Nardo*, pp. 146-47.
6. Ramón Gómez de la Serna, *Las tres gracias* (Madrid: Editorial Perseo, 1949), prol., p. 28.
7. *Ibid.*, p. 201.
8. *Ibid.*, p. 258.
9. Ramón Gómez de la Serna, *Piso bajo* (Madrid: Espasa Calpe, 1961), prologue, p. 7.
10. Antonio Valencia, "Ley de la novela de Ramón," *Arriba* (Madrid), April 15, 1962, p. 23.
11. Carlos Fernández Cuenca, "En *El hombre perdido* plantea Ramón Gómez de la Serna la novela de la nebulosa y del azar," *Correo Literario* (Madrid) IV (1953), 16.
12. Ramón Gómez de la Serna, *Obras selectas* (Madrid: Editorial Plenitud, 1947), p. 1090.
13. *Ibid.*, p. 1092.
14. Ramón Gómez de la Serna, *El incongruente* (Madrid: Espasa Calpe, 1922), p. 81.
15. Ramón Gómez de la Serna, *El hombre perdido* (Buenos Aires: Editorial Poseidón, 1947), pp. 7-16.
16. *Ibid.*, p. 215.
17. *Ibid.*, p. 221.
18. *Ibid.*, p. 41.
19. Ramón Gómez de la Serna, *!Rebeca!* (Santiago de Chile: Editorial Ercilla, 1936), p. 72
20. *Ibid.*, p. 193.

Chapter Four

1. Ramón Gómez de la Serna, "La tormenta," *La malicia de las acacias; Novelas* (Valencia: Editorial Sempere, 1924), p. 121.
2. Ramón Gómez de la Serna, "De otra raza," *La malicia de las acacias; Novelas*, p. 202.

3. Ramón Gómez de la Serna, *Seis falsas novelas* (Paris: Editorial Mundial, 1927), prol., p. 8.
4. *Ibid.*, prologue, p. 11.
5. Ramón Gómez de la Serna, "La fúnebre," *Seis falsas novelas,* p. 72.
6. Ramón Gómez de la Serna, "El dueño del átomo," *El dueño del átomo; Novelas* (Madrid: Editorial Biblioteca Nueva, 1928), p. 31.
7. Ramón Gómez de la Serna, "El regalo del doctor," *La hiperestésica* (Madrid: Editorial Ulises, 1934), p. 310.
8. *Ibid.*
9. It has been impossible to trace the movie to discover whether it preceded Ramón's story or appeared later.
10. Ramón Gómez de la Serna, *Doña Juana la loca; Novelas superhistóricas* (Buenos Aires: Editorial Clydoc, 1944) prologue, p. 10.
11. *Ibid.*, p. 59.
12. *Ibid.*, p. 157.
13. Ramón Gómez de la Serna, *Cuentos del fin del año* (Madrid: Editorial Clan, 1947), p. 9.
14. *Ibid.*, p. 35.
15. *Ibid.*, p. 39.
16. *Ibid.*, p. 108.

Chapter Five

1. Ramón Gómez de la Serna, *Pombo* (Madrid: Imprenta Mesón de Paños, 1918). The pages in this edition of *Pombo* are not numbered. All citations in this paragraph are from this edition.
2. Ramón Gómez de la Serna, *Goya* (Madrid: Ediciones La Nave, 1928), p. 86. Hereafter referred to as *Goya.*
3. *Ibid.*, p. 92.
4. *Ibid.*, p. 88.
5. Lucio Ambruzzi, "Goya attraverso Ramón," *Convivium* (Genoa Torino), I (1929), 724.
6. Ramón Gómez de la Serna, *Biografías completas* (Madrid: Aguilar, 1959), p. 1378.
7. *Ibid.*, p. 1394.
8. Ramón Gómez de la Serna, "Darío de Regoyos," *Nuevos retratos contemporáneos* (Buenos Aires: Editorial Sudamericana, 1945), p. 221. Hereafter referred to as *N.R.C.* Names of biographical sketches from this work will be indicated in the citation, when not clearly specified in the text.
9. *Ibid.*, p. 217.
10. Ramón Gómez de la Serna, "Lhotismo," *Ismos* (Madrid: Biblioteca Nueva, 1931), p. 40. Hereafter referred to as *Ismos*. Names of specific biographical sketches from this work will be indicated, when not clearly specified in the text.
11. *Ibid.*, p. 369.

12. José Ortega y Gasset, *El Espectador*, II (Madrid: *Revista de Occidente*, 1963), 74.
13. The novel was ¡*Rebeca!*, written earlier, but not published until 1936. The biographical works mentioned are indicated in the continuation of the text.
14. Alfredo Cardona Peña, "Ramón, los clásicos y otros poemas," *La Nueva Democracia* (New York), XXXVIII (1958), 79. The author points out that on p. 42 of *Lope viviente*, Ramón states that Lope's neighbors included Cervantes, Quevedo, Góngora, and Don Leandro Fernández de Moratin, thereby committing a gross error of two centuries, as Moratin was born in 1760, Lope in 1562. The offending sentence is deleted from the 1959 edition of Ramón's biography of Lope which appears in *Biografías completas*.
15. Ramón Gómez de la Serna, *José Gutiérrez Solana* (Buenos Aires: Editorial Poseidón, 1944), p. 180.
16. Ramón Gómez de la Serna, *Don Ramón María del Valle-Inclán* (Buenos Aires: Espasa-Calpe Argentina, Colección Austral, 1942), p. 135. Hereafter referred to as *V.I.*
17. Melchor Fernández Almagro, "La generación unipersonal de Gómez de la Serna," *España* (Madrid), March 24, 1923, p. 11.
18. *V.I.*, p. 135.
19. Ramón Gómez de la Serna, *Retratos contemporáneos* (Buenos Aires: Editorial Sudamericana, 1941), p. 9. Hereafter referred to as *R. contemp.* Names of specific biographical sketches from this work will be indicated, when not clearly specified in the text.
20. *Ibid.*, p. 10.
21. *Ibid.*, pp. 160-61.
22. *Ibid.*, p. 161.
23. *N.R.C.*, p. 234.
24. *Ibid.*, p. 244.
25. Ramón Gómez de la Serna, "Enrique Larreta," *Retratos completos* (Madrid: Aguilar, 1961), p. 1187. Hereafter referred to as *R.C.* Names of specific biographical sketches from this work will be indicated, when not clearly specified in the text. This is the first collection of sketches which contains Larreta's biography.
26. *R. contemp.*, pp. 126-27.
27. *N.R.C.*, p. 192.
28. *Ibid.*, p. 55.
29. Perhaps his awareness of loneliness was also deepened by his increasing isolation in Buenos Aires.
30. *R. contemp.*, p. 405.
31. *Ibid.*, pp. 421-22.
32. *N.R.C.*, p. 290.
33. *Ibid.*, p. 245.
34. *Ibid.*, p. 252.

35. *Ibid.*, pp. 250-52.
36. *Ibid.*, p. 297.
37. *Ibid.*, p. 258.
38. *R. contemp.*, p. 51.
39. *Ibid.*, p. 44.
40. *Ibid.*, p. 47.
41. *Ibid.*, p. 380.
42. *N.R.C.*, p. 99.
43. Ramón Gómez de la Serna, *Nuevas páginas de mi vida* (Valencia: Editorial Marfil, 1957), pp. 69-70. Hereafter referred to as *N. pág.*
44. *N.R.C.*, p. 69.
45. *R. contemp.*, p. 10.
46. Gaspar Gómez de la Serna, *Ramón* (Madrid: Taurus Ediciones, 1963), pp. 219-20.
47. *Ibid.*, p. 219.
48. *Ibid.*, pp. 219-20.
49. *R.C.*, p. 913.
50. Ramón Gómez de la Serna, *Automoribundia* (Buenos Aires: Editorial Sudamericana, 1948), p. 392. Hereafter referred to as *Auto.*
51. Ramón Gómez de la Serna, *Lope de Vega* (Buenos Aires: Editorial la Universidad, 1945), p. 80. Hereafter referred to as *Lope.*
52. *Auto.*, p. 9.
53. *Ibid.*, p. 15.
54. *Ibid.*, p. 16.
55. *Ibid.*, p. 12.
56. *Ibid.*, p. 9.
57. *Ibid.*, p. 744.
58. Rodolfo Cardona, *Ramón, A Study of Gómez de la Serna and His Works* (New York: Eliseo Torres and Sons, 1957), p. 92. Hereafter referred to as *Ramón.*
59. *Auto.*, p. 652.
60. Cardona, *Ramón*, p. 106.
61. Ramón Gómez de la Serna, *Cartas a mí mismo* (Barcelona: Editorial AHR, 1956), p. 27. Hereafter referred to as *Cartas.*
62. *Ibid.*, p. 35.
63. *Ibid.*, p. 48.
64. *Ibid.*, p. 56.
65. *Ibid.*, p. 130.
66. *Ibid.*, p. 131.
67. *Auto.*, p. 764.
68. *N. pag.*, p. 8.
69. *Ibid.*, pp. 82-83.
70. *Ibid.*, p. 83.
71. *Ibid.*, pp. 86-87.
72. *Ibid.*, p. 71.

73. *Ibid.*, p. 8.
74. *Ibid.*, p. 154.
75. *Ibid.*, p. 127.
76. *Ibid.*, p. 128.
77. *Ibid.*, p. 232.

Chapter Six

1. Most of the manuscripts left by Ramón Gómez de la Serna were sold by his widow Luisa Sofovich to the University of Pittsburgh, Pennsylvania; all the manuscripts and papers discussed here are the property of the University of Pittsburgh Libraries, Special Collections Department and are quoted by permission of the University of Pittsburgh. All rights reserved.
2. Pedro Massa, a well-known journalist with *La Nación* in Buenos Aires, and Spanish correspondent for *ABC* from Buenos Aires, states this in an unpublished article which he provided to this writer, saying: "When he went along the street . . . he would stop suddenly, and jot some words in a notebook he carried for that purpose. . . ." p. 4.
3. Both Massa and Jorge Luis Borges who had known Ramón in his youth in Madrid, and again in his maturer years in Buenos Aires, said in personal interviews with this author (Borges, Dec. 18, 19, 1972; Massa, Dec. 21, 1972) that Ramón drank profusely. As his loneliness and frustrations increased, as his health deteriorated, as his financial pressures increased, as writing began to require increasing effort, he drank more. Perhaps, too, like Poe, he may have sought the marginally conscious state by drinking sufficiently to induce it.
4. Massa, in the unpublished article cited above, which he provided to this writer (Dec. 21, 1972), described how these works, unsuspected even by Luisa, were accidentally found as Ramón lay dying.
5. It is in the possession of the Special Collections section of the library at the University of Pittsburgh, as indicated above. Some are currently being studied for doctoral dissertations with the hope of eventual publication by their researchers.

Chapter Seven

1. Hernani Rossi, "Comentarios al mejor libro del mes," *La Gaceta Literaria* (Madrid), V (October 1, 1931), 16.
2. Luis Cernuda, "Gómez de la Serna y la generación poética del 1925," *Estudios sobre poesía contemporánea* (Madrid: Ediciones Guadarrama, 1957), p. 165.
3. Ramón Gómez de la Serna, *Total de greguerías* (Madrid: Aguilar, 1955), pp. xxvi-xxviii. Hereafter referred to as *Tot. gregs.*
4. Ramón Gómez de la Serna, *Automoribundia* (Buenos Aires: Editorial Sudamericana, 1948), p. 641. Hereafter referred to as *Auto.*

5. Ramón Gómez de la Serna, "María Mallo," *Retratos completos* (Madrid: Aguilar, 1961), p. 1127. Hereafter referred to as *R.C.*
6. Ramón Gómez de la Serna, *Edgar Poe, el genio de América* (Buenos Aires: Editorial Losada, 1957), p. 31. Hereafter referred to as *Poe.*
7. "Wilde," *R.C.,* p. 920.
8. Ramón Gómez de la Serna, "Falla," *Nuevos retratos contemporáneos* (Buenos Aires: Editorial Sudamericana, 1945), p. 311. Hereafter referred to as *N.R.C.*
9. "Neruda," *N.R.C.,* p. 271.
10. Ramón Gómez de la Serna, *Goya* (Madrid: Ediciones La Nave, 1928), p. 86. Hereafter referred to as *Goya.*
11. Ramón Gómez de la Serna, *Lope viviente* (Buenos Aires: Espasa-Calpe Argentina, Colección Austral, 1954), p. 38. The line cited here does not appear in the original 1945 edition entitled *Lope de Vega.* It first appears in the 1954 edition. In subsequent references, *Lope viviente* will be referred to as *Lope.*
12. Ramón Gómez de la Serna, *Don Ramón María del Valle-Inclán* (Buenos Aires: Espasa-Calpe Argentina, Colección Austral, 1942), p. 83. Hereafter referred to as *V.I.*
13. Ramón Gómez de la Serna, *Don Diego Valázquez* (Buenos Aires: Editorial Poseidón, Colección Biblioteca Argentina de Arte, 1943), p. 43. Hereafter referred to as *Velázquez.*
14. Ramón Gómez de la Serna, *Azorín* (Madrid: Editorial La Nave, 1923), p. 55. Hereafter referred to as *Azorín.*
15. Ramón Gómez de la Serna, "Colette," *Retratos contemporáneos* (Buenos Aires: Editorial Sudamericana, 1941), p. 439. Hereafter referred to as *R. contemp.*
16. "Kafka," *N.R.C.,* p. 236.
17. *Tot. gregs.,* p. 92.
18. *Ibid.,* p. 469.
19. Carlos Murciano, "La vida, esa greguería," *Punta Europa* (Madrid), LXXXI (1963), 25.
20. *N.R.C.,* p. 777.
21. *R. Contemp.* p. 402.
22. *N.R.C.,* p. 302.
23. *R.C., p. 1122.*
24. *Auto.,* p. 555.
25. Good examples of such images may also be found in the following works: roosters in "Marinetti" *(Ismos,* p. 107); cats in "Colette" *(R. contemp.,* p. 433); tigers in "Ruiz Contreras" *(R. contemp.,* p. 133); lions in "Noel" *(R. contemp.,* p. 66); onagers in "Unamuno" (R. contemp., p. 403); serpents in *"Valle-Inclán,"* p. 178; deer in "Nerval" *(Efigies,* p. 164); fish in "Pirandello" *(N.R.C.,* p. 13) and in "Colette" *(R. contemp.,* p. 435); marine monsters in "Gourmont" *(R. contemp.,* p. 185); satyrs in "Keyserling" *(R. contemp.,* p. 76); dragons, "Keyserling" *(R. contemp.,* p. 77).

26. Rafael María Hornedo, "El catolicismo de Ramón Gómez de la Serna," *Razón y fe* (Madrid), CLXVII (1963), 349.
27. Ramón Gómez de la Serna, "Picassismo," *Ismos* (Madrid: Biblioteca Nueva, 1931), p. 101. Hereafter referred to as *Ismos*.
28. "Cami," *R. contemp.*, p. 267.
29. "Macedonio Fernández," *R. contemp.*, p. 157.
30. *Auto.*, p. 459.
31. *V.I.*, p. 135.
32. Angel del Río, and M.J. Benardete, "Ramón Gómez de la Serna," *El concepto contemporáneo de España: Antología de ensayos (1895-1931)* (Buenos Aires: Editorial Losada, 1946), p. 715.
33. *Azorín*, pp. 38-39.
34. *Poe*, p. 48.
35. "Picassismo," *Ismos*, p. 101.
36. José María Salaverría, "Un escritor" reprinted in *Libro nuevo* by Ramón Gómez de la Serna (Madrid: Imprenta Mesón de Paños, 1929), p. 34.
37. *V.I.*, p. 128.
38. *Azorín*, p. 242.
39. "Wilde," *R.C.*, p. 882.
40. *Tot. gregs.*, p. xxiii.
41. Juan Corominas, *Diccionario crítico etimológico de la lengua castellana, II* (Madrid: Editorial Gredos, 1954) p. 784.
42. *Tot. gregs.*, p. xxiii.
43. *Ibid.*, p. xxv.
44. *Ibid.*, p. xxxi.
45. *Ibid.*, p. xxxiv.
46. *Ibid.*, p. xlv.
47. *Ibid.*, p. xxxv.
48. *Ibid.*, p. li.
49. *Ibid.*, pp. xxxvii-xlii.
50. Rafael Cansinos Asséns, *La Nueva literatura, IV: La evolución de la novela, 1917-1927,* (Madrid: V.H. de Sanz Callejo, 1927), p. 364.
51. "Vives," *N.R.C.*, p. 121.
52. Pedro Salinas, "Escorzo de Ramón," *Literatura española siglo XX* (Mexico, D.F.: Editorial Séneca, 1941), p. 244.
53. Tomás Borrás, "El descubridor de continentes inéditos en el mar del castellano," *Revista de ideas estéticas* (Madrid), XXI (1963), 30.
54. Gaspar Gómez de la Serna, "Hacia el concepto de la greguería," *Papeles de Son Armadáns* (Mallorca), XXX (1963), 199.
55. Luis Cernuda, "Gómez de la Serna y la generación poética del 1925," *Estudios sobre Poesía contemporánea* (Madrid: Guadarrama, 1957), pp. 174-75.
56. "Mallo," *R.C.*, p. 1128.
57. *R.C.*, p. 929.

58. "Cocteau," *Ismos*, p. 358.
59. *Azorín*, p. 359.
60. "d'Ors," *R. contemp.*, p. 359.
61. Ramón Gómez de la Serna, *Mi Tía Carolina Coronado* (Buenos Aires: Emecé Editores, 1942), p. 15.
62. *Poe*, p. 117.
63. *Goya*, p. 80.
64. E. García-Luengo, "Escritor muy personal," *Indice de Artes y Letras* (Madrid), LXXXVI (1955), n.p.
65. *Goya*, p. 90.
66. *Ibid.*, p. 86.
67. *Velá*zquez, p. 43.
68. *R. contemp.*, p. 25.
69. Ramón Gómez de la Serna, *Efigies* (Madrid: Ediciones Oriente, 1929), p. 9.
70. *N.R.C.*, p. 105.
71. *Ibid.*, p. 298.
72. *Ismos*, p. 258.
73. Ramón Gómez de la Serna, *Quevedo* (Buenos Aires: Espasa-Calpe Argentina, Colección Austral, 1953), p. 14.
74. *Efigies*, p. 163.
75. *Azorín*, p. 163.
76. *V.I.*, p. 26.
77. This line does not appear in the original 1930 edition of *Azorín*. It can be found in *Biografías completas*, p. 1317, and first appeared in the epilogue which was added to the work in 1942.
78. *Tot. gregs.*, p. xxix.
79. *Ibid.*, p. xxxi.
80. *Ibid.*; p. 1.
81. Rafael Calleja, "Ramón: A propósito de *El torero Caracho*," *Revista de Occidente* XVI (1927), 381.
82. Cardona, *Ramón*, p. 145.
83. Guillermo de Torre, "Gómez de la Serna: Medio siglo de literatura," *Clavileño* (Madrid), XXI (1955), 11.
84. Ramón Gómez de la Serna, "Las palabras y lo indecible," *Lo cursi y otros ensayos* (Buenos Aires: Editorial Sudamericana, 1943), pp. 191-204.
85. Francisco Ynduraín, "Sobre el arte de Ramón," *Revista de Ideas Estéticas* (Madrid), XXI (1963), 40.
86. Ricardo Senabre Sempere, "Sobre la técnica de la greguería," *Papeles de Son Armadáns* (Mallorca), XLV, num. 134, 125.
87. *Ibid.*, pp. 132-35.
88. Ramón Gómez de la Serna, *El Greco* (Madrid: Ediciones Nuestra Raza, 1935), p. 134.
89. *Lope*, p. 186.
90. "Echegaray," *N.R.C.*, p. 68.

91. *N.R.C.*, p. 226.
92. *Quevedo*, p. 61.
93. *Azorín*, p. 234.
94. On Sawa, in *V.I.*, p. 39.
95. *Greco.*, p. 78.
96. *Poe*, p. 86.
97. "Kafka," *N.R.C.*, p. 237.
98. *V.I.*, p. 59.
99. *Azorín*, p. 89.
100. *Poe*, p. 87.
101. "Mallo," *R.C.*, p. 1138.
102. "Aleixandre," *R.C.*, p. 1175.
103. "Vives," *N.R.C.*, p. 126.
104. "Mesa," *N.R.C.*, p. 196.
105. "Apollinaire," *Ismos*, p. 37.
106. "Shaw," *N.R.C.*, p. 257.
107. "Unamuno," *R. contemp.*, p. 407.
108. "Pirandello," *N.R.C.*, p. 23.
109. "Macedonio Fernández," *R. contemp.*, p. 158.
110. *Poe*, p. 116.
111. *Quevedo*, p. 30.
112. "Marinetti," *Ismos*, p. 122.
113. Carlos Bousoño, *Teoría de la expresión literaria* (Madrid: Editorial Gredos, 1956), p. 218.
114. "Vives," *N.R.C.*, p. 126.
115. *Lope*, p. 50.
116. *V.I.*, pp. 52-53.
117. *Quevedo*, p. 30.
118. *Velázquez*, p. 43.
119. "Pérez Galdós," *N.R.C.*, p. 209.
120. *N.R.C.*, p. 303.
121. "Echegaray," *N.R.C.*, p. 67.
122. *V.I.*, p. 144.
123. *Azorín*, p. 54.
124. José María Salaverría, "Un escritor," reprinted by Ramón Gómez de la Serna in *Libro nuevo* (Madrid: Imprenta Mesón de Paños, 1920), p. 34.
125. "Juan Ramón Jiménez," *R. contemp.*, p. 20.
126. *V.I.*, p. 59.
127. "Ehrenburgh," *R. contemp.*, pp. 355-56.
128. "Nerval," *Efigies*, p. 181.
129. Gonzalo Torrente Ballester, "Gómez de la Serna," *Panorama de la literatura española contemporánea, I*, 2nd. edition (Madrid: Ediciones Guadarrama, 1961), p. 278.
130. Juan Chabás, "Ramón Gómez de la Serna," *Literatura española contemporánea, 1898-1950* (Havana: Editorial Cultural, 1952), p. 384.

131. José María Salaverría, "Un escritor," reprinted in *Libro nuevo*, p. 34.
132. *R. contemp.*, pp. 203-8.
133. *R.C.*, p. 898.

Chapter Eight

1. Luis Cernuda, "Gómez de la Serna y la generación poética del 1925," *Estudios sobre poesía contemporánea* (Madrid: Ediciones Guadarrama, 1957), p. 165.

Selected Bibliography

PRIMARY SOURCES

Works of Ramón Gómez de la Serna

The list to follow is far from exhaustive. It is arranged alphabetically by title. The most complete bibliography available of his writings may be found in Gaspar Gómez de la Serna, cited below, among the SECONDARY SOURCES.

El alba (Madrid: Editorial Saturnino Calleja, 1918).
"La abandonada en el Rastro," *Revista de Occidente* (Madrid), XXIII, 1929.
"Aventuras y desgracias de un sinsombrerista," *Revista de Occidente* (Madrid), XXXV, 1932.
Automoribundia (Buenos Aires: Editorial Sudamericana, 1948).
Azorín (Madrid: Editorial La Nave, 1923, 1930. Also Buenos Aires: Editorial Losada, 1942, 1948, 1950).
La bailarina (Madrid: Imprenta Aurora, Sociedad de Autores Españoles, 1911).
Biografías completas (Madrid: Aguilar, 1959). Contents: "Autorretrato de Ramón Gómez de la Serna," "El Greco," "Lope viviente," "Quevedo," "Don Diego Velázquez," "Goya," "Edgar Poe," "Mi tía Carolina Coronado," "Don Ramón María del Valle-Inclán," "Azorín," and "José Gutiérrez Solana."
El caballero del hongo gris (Paris, Madrid and Lisbon: Editorial Agencia Mundial de Librería, 1928. Also, Madrid: Revista Literaria: Novelas y Cuentos, 1936, and Buenos Aires: L. Mera, 1941).
"La capa de Don Dámaso," *Revista de Occidente* (Madrid), V, 1924.
Caprichos (Madrid: Editorial La Lectura, 1925).
Cartas a las golondrinas (Barcelona: Editorial Juventud, 1949).
Cartas a mí mismo (Barcelona: Editorial AHR, 1956).
El chalet de las rosas (Valencia: Editorial Sempere, 1924. Also Barcelona: José Janés, 1948).
Cinelandia (Valencia: Editorial Sempere, 1923).
El circo (Madrid: Imprenta Latina, 1917. Also Valencia: Editorial Sempere, 1924 and Barcelona: Editorial Lauro, 1943).

El cólera azul (Buenos Aires: Sur, 1937). Contents: "El cólera azul," "Peluquería feliz," "La estufa de cristal," "La niña Alcira, "El defensor del cementerio," "Suspensión del destino," "Destrozonas," "Las consignatarias," "Se presentó el hígado," "Ella + Ella - El + El," "Pueblo de morenas."
"Las cosas y 'el ello,' " *Revista de Occidente* (Madrid), XLV (1934), 190-208.
Cuento de Calleja: Drama (Madrid: Imprenta de J. Fernández Arias, Sociedad de Autores Españoles, 1909).
Cuentos de fin de año (Madrid: Editorial Clan, 1947). Contents: "Olvido," "Nochebuena del año dos mil quinientos," "Cena de académicos," "La botella y el candelabro," "La tía Marta," "El gabán de nieve," "El pandero de Rosaura," "El natalicio del poeta," "El creador de nacimientos," "Cuento de navidad con vidriera de colores."
Cuentos para niños (Madrid: Editorial Calpe, 1924). Contents: "En el bazar más suntuoso del mundo," "El marquesito en el circo," "Por los tejados."
Lo cursi y otros ensayos (Buenos Aires: Editorial Sudamericana, 1943).
"Las danzas de pasión," *Prometeo* (Madrid), 1911.
"Desolación," *Ateneo* (Madrid), 1909.
Diario póstumo. Edited by Luisa Sofovich (Barcelona: Plaza y Janés, S.A., 1972).
Disparates (Madrid: Calpe, Colección "Los Humoristas," 1921).
El doctor inverosímil (Madrid: La Novela de Bolsillo, 1914. Also Madrid: Atenea, 1921, Buenos Aires: Editorial Losada, 1941, 1948 and Madrid: Aguilar, 1948).
Don Diego Velázquez (Buenos Aires: Editorial Poseidón, Colección Biblioteca Argentina de Arte, 1943).
Don Ramón María del Valle-Inclán (Buenos Aires: Espasa-Calpe Argentina, Colección Austral, 1942, 1944, 1947).
Doña Juana la loca; Novelas superhistóricas (Buenos Aires: Editorial Clydoc, 1944. Also Madrid: Revista de Occidente, 1944, 1950). Contents: "Doña Juana la loca," "El caballero de Olmedo," "Doña Urraca de Castilla," "Los siete infantes de Lara," "La emparedada de Burgos," "La Beltraneja," and "Los adelantados."
"Los dos espejos," *Prometeo* (Madrid), 1911.
El drama del palacio deshabitado; Dramas (Madrid: Editorial América, 1926). Contents: "El drama del palacio deshabitado," "La utopía," "Beatriz," "La corona de hierro," and "El lunático."
El dueño del átomo; Novelas (Madrid: Editorial Biblioteca Nueva, 1928. Also Buenos Aires: Editorial Losada, 1945, 1948). Contents: "El dueño del átomo," "La casa triangular," "El Ruso," "El gran griposo," "La hija del verano," "El hombre de la galería," "La saturada," "El olor de las mimosas," "El hombre de los pies grandes."
Edgar Poe (Madrid: Biblioteca Nueva, 1920). Revised edition: *Edgar Poe, genio de América* (Buenos Aires: Editorial Losada, 1953).

Efigies (Madrid: Ediciones Oriente, 1929. Also Madrid: Aguilar; 1945). Contents: "El desgarrado Baudelaire," "Retrato del gran mariscal Barbey d Aurevilly," "Retrato del Conde Villiers de l'Isle-Adam," "El suicida, Gerardo de Nerval," and "Ruskin el apasionado."
Entrando en fuego (Segovia: Imprenta del Diario de Avisos, 1905).
Las escaleras (Madrid: Editorial Cruz y Raya, 1935).
Ex-votos; Dramas (Madrid: Imprenta Aurora, 1910). Contents: "Los sonámbulos," "Siempreviva," "La casa nueva," "Los unánimes," "Tránsito," "Fiesta de Dolores," "La corona de hierro," "La utopía."
Gollerías (Valencia: Editorial Sempere, 1926. Also, Buenos Aires: Editorial Losada, 1946). Later edition includes *Ramonismo,* and *Variaciones.*
Goya (Madrid: Ediciones La Nave, 1928, Also, Santiago de Chile: Editorial Ercilla, 1937, Buenos Aires: Editorial Poseidón, 1942. Buenos Aires: Espasa-Calpe Argentina, Colección Austral, 1948, 1950).
El gran hotel (Madrid: Editorial América, 1922. Also Barcelona: Editorial Lauro, 1944, Buenos Aires: Editorial Losada, 1944, and Barcelona: Editorial Janés, 1946).
"Gravedad e importancia del humorismo," *Revista de Occidente* (Madrid), XXVIII (1930), 348-91.
El Greco (Madrid: Ediciones Nuestra Raza, 1935. Also Madrid: Nuestra Raza, 1935, Santiago de Chile: Editorial Ercilla, 1938, and Buenos Aires: Editorial Losada, 1950).
Greguerías (Valencia: Editorial Prometeo, 1917. Also Buenos Aires: Espasa-Calpe Argentina, Colección Austral, 1940, 1943, 1945, 1952, 1953). *Greguerías completas* (Barcelona: Editorial Lauro, 1947), and *Total de Greguerías* (Madrid: Aguilar, 1955).
"El hijo surrealista," *Revista de Occidente* (Madrid), XXX, 1930.
La hiperestésica; Novelas (Madrid: Editorial Ulises, 1934). Contents: "La hiperestésica," "El regalo del doctor," "El vegetariano," and "La roja."
El hombre perdido (Buenos Aires: Editorial Poseidón, 1947).
El incongruente (Madrid: Espasa-Calpe, 1922. Also Buenos Aires: Editorial Losada, 1946).
Ismos (Madrid: Biblioteca Nueva, 1931. Also Buenos Aires: Editorial Poseidón, 1943). Contents: "Apollinerismo," "Picassismo," "Futurismo," "Negrismo," "Luminismo," "Klaxismo," "Estantiferismo," "Toulouselautrecismo," "Monstruosismo," "Archipenkismo," "Maquinismo," "Lhoteísmo," "Simultaneísmo," "Jazzbandismo," "Humorismo," "Lipchitzmo," "Tubularismo," "Ninfismo," "Dadaísmo," "Charlotismo," "Suprarrealismo," "Botellismo," "Riverismo," "Novelismo," and "Serafismo." The 1943 edition contained also "Ducassismo," and "Daliísmo."
José Gutiérrez Solana (Buenos Aires: Editorial Poseidón, 1944).
"El laberinto," *Prometeo* (Madrid), 1910.
Leopoldo y Teresa (Madrid: La Novela Corta, 1922).
El libro nuevo (Madrid: Imprenta Mesón de Paños, 1920).
Lope de Vega (Buenos Aires: Editorial La Universidad, 1945). Later pub-

lished as *Lope viviente* (Buenos Aires: Espasa-Calpe Argentina, Colección Austral, 1954).
"Madrid," *La Tribuna*, 1920.
La malicia de las acacias; Novelas (Valencia: Editorial Sempere, 1924). Contents: "La malicia de las acacias," "Los gemelos y el guante," "El joven de las sobremesas," "La tormenta," "La Gallipava," "Miedo al mar," "De otra raza," "La Gangosa," and "Aquella novela."
"Los medios seres," *Revista de Occidente* (Madrid), XXVI (1929), 85-120 and 348-93 Also (Madrid: Editorial Prensa Moderna, 1929, Buenos Aires: Editorial Poseidón, 1943).
Mi tía Carolina Coronado (Buenos Aires: Emecé Editores, 1942).
Morbideces (Madrid: Imprenta, "El trabajo," 1908). Contents: "Morbideces," "El ciego y la hetaira," "El apestado," "La doncella," "La muerte del lunático," and "La caja de Pandora."
Los muertos, las muertas y otras fantasmagorías (Madrid: Ediciones "El Arbol," Editorial Cruz y Raya, 1935. Also, Madrid: Espasa-Calpe, Colección Austral, 1942, 1944, 1961).
Muestrarios (Madrid: Biblioteca Nueva, 1918).
La mujer de ámbar (Madrid: Biblioteca Nueva, 1927. Also, Buenos Aires: Editorial Espasa-Calpe Argentina, Colección Austral, 1937, 1945, 1948).
La Nardo (Madrid: Editorial Ulises, 1930. Also Santiago de Chile, Editorial Ercilla, 1944, Barcelona: Editorial José Janés, 1950).
Nostalgias de Madrid (Madrid: Editorial El Grifón de Plata, 1956).
El novelista (Valencia: Editorial Sempere, 1923. Also, Madrid: Atenea, 1923, Madrid: Editorial América, 1925, Buenos Aires: Editorial Poseidón, 1946).
Nuevas páginas de mi vida (Valencia: Editorial Marfil, 1957).
Nuevos retratos contemporáneos (Buenos Aires: Editorial Sudamericana, 1945). Contents: "Pirandello," "Los Machado-Manuel," "Los Machado-Antonio," "Ibsen," "Ventura Garcia Calderón," "Don José Echegaray," "Bontempelli y Pitigrilli," "Benavente," "Adriano Del Valle," "Amadeo Vives," "Vicente Blasco Ibáñez," "Emilia Pardo Bazán," "José Pijoán," "Pedro Luis de Gálvez," "Enrique de Mesa," "Pérez Galdós," "Darío de Regoyos," "Marcos Chagall," "Kafka," "Bartrina," "Bernard Shaw," "Pablo Neruda," "Gabriel Miró," "Pedro de Répide," "Cansinos Asséns," and "Manuel de Falla."
Obras Completas, I (Barcelona: Editorial AHR, 1956). Contents: "El Rastro," "El drama del palacio deshabitado," "La utopía," "Beatriz," "La corona de hierro," "El lunático," "Gollerías," "El alba," "Goya," "El Greco," "Azorín," "Mi tía Carolina Coronado," "La viuda blanca y negra," "La mujer de ámbar," "La hiperestésica," "El regalo al Doctor," "La quinta de Palmyra," "El gran hotel," "Cinelandia," "Leopoldo y Teresa," "El turco de los nardos," and "Aventura y desgracia de un sinsombrerista."
Obras Completas, II (Barcelona: Editorial AHR, 1957). Contents: "Introducción," "Ramón y Picasso," by Guillermo de Torre, and "Pombo,"

Selected Bibliography

"Efigies," "El circo," "Trampantojos," "Ismos," "Don Ramón María del Valle-Inclán," "José Gutiérrez Solana," "Retratos contemporáneos," "El caballero del hongo gris," 'El torero Caracho," and "Policéfalo y Señora."
Obras selectas (Madrid: Editorial Plenitud, 1947). Contents: "El secreto del acueducto," "El dueño del átomo," "El cólera azul," "La niña Alcira," "Pueblo de morenas," "El turco de los nardos," "El doctor inverosímil," "El regalo del doctor," "María Yarsilovna," "Los dos marineros," "La virgen pintada de rojo," "Doña Juana la loca," "El caballero de Olmedo," "La emparedada de Burgos," "Los medios seres," "Escaleras," "Greguerías," "Las chimeneas," "El éxito del sifón," "La almohada de viaje," "Los árboles de los bastos," "lo cursi," "Senos," "El circo," "Otras fantasmagorías," "El alba," "Solana y otros pintores," "El Greco," "Don Diego Velázquez," "Goya," "Picassismo," "Cartas a las golondrinas," "El hombre perdido," "Palacio del psicoanálisis," "Pirandello," "Los Machado," "Azorín," "Madrid," "Cosas de Pombo," and "El Rastro."
Oscar Wilde (Madrid: Biblioteca Nueva, 1921. Also Buenos Aires: Editorial Poseidón, 1944).
Páginas escogidas e inéditas de Silverio Lanza, "In memoriam" and "Epílogo" by Ramón (Madrid: Biblioteca Nueva, 1918).
"Las palabras y lo indecible," *Revista de Occidente* (Madrid), LI, 1936.
Piso bajo (Madrid: Espasa-Calpe, 1961).
Policéfalo y señora (Madrid: Espasa-Calpe, 1932. Also Santiago de Chile Editorial Ercilla, 1936, 1940, 1944).
Pombo (Madrid: Imprenta Mesón de Paños, 1918).
Pombo, La sagrada cripta de Pombo (Madrid: Imprenta Mesón de Panōs, 1924).
El Prado (Madrid: Librería, 1925).
Quevedo (Buenos Aires: Espasa-Calpe Argentina, Colección Austral, 1953).
La quinta de Palmyra (Madrid: Editorial Biblioteca Nueva, 1923. Also Buenos Aires: Editorial Losada, 1944).
Ramonismo (Madrid: Calpe, Colección "Los Humoristas," 1923).
El Rastro (Valencia: Sociedad Editorial Prometeo, 1915. Also, Madrid: Ediciones La Nave, 1931, Madrid: Editorial Atenea, 1933).
¡Rebeca! (Santiago de Chile: Editorial Ercilla, 1936. Also, Barcelona: Editorial Janés, 1947).
Retratos completos (Madrid: Aguilar, 1961). Contents: "Efigies," "Retratos contemporáneos," "Nuevos retratos contemporáneos," and "Otros retratos," which comprise: "Isidore Ducasse," "Oscar Wilde," "Toulouse-Lautrec," "Saint-Paul Roux," "Marinetti," "Guillermo Apollinaire," "Jean Cocteau," "Marie Laurencín," "Lipchitz," "Charlot," "Pablo Picasso," "Diego Rivera," "Juan Echevarría," "Juan Gris," "Salvador Dalí," "María Gutiérrez Blanchard," "Maruja Mallo," "Norah Borges," "Jardiel Poncela," "Vicente Aleixandre," "Gerardo Diego," "Salvador Bartolozzi," and "Enrique Larreta."

Retratos contemporáneos (Buenos Aires: Editorial Sudamericana, 1941, 1944). Contents: "Juan Ramón Jiménez," "Eugenio Noel," "El Conde de Keyserling," "Oliverio Girondo," "Jean Cassou," "Francisco Vighi," "Paul Morand," "Luis Ruiz Contreras," "Santiago Rusiñol," "Mac-Orlan," "Macedonio Fernández," "Remy de Gourmont," "Miss Barney," "Fernando Villalón," "Emilio Carrère," "Antonio de Hoyos," "Mauricio Maeterlinck," "Cami," "Don Ramón del Valle-Inclán," "Ilya Ehrenburg," "Eugenio D'Ors," "Pío Baroja," "Don Miguel de Unamumo," and "Colette."

El secreto del acueducto (Madrid: Biblioteca Nueva, 1922).

Seis falsas novelas (Paris: Editorial Mundial, 1927. Also, Buenos Aires: Editorial Losada, 1943). Contents: "María Yarsilovna," "Los dos marineros," "La fúnebre," "La virgen pintada de rojo," "La mujer vestido de hombre," and "El hijo del millonario."

Senos (Madrid: Imprenta Latina, 1917. Also, Segovia: Beltrán, 1923).

"Teatro en soledad," *Prometeo* (Madrid), 1912.

Toda la historia de la Puerta del Sol (Madrid: La Tribuna, 1920).

El torero Caracho (Paris, Madrid, and Lisbon: Editorial Agencia Mundial de Librería, 1926. Also, Mexico: Gibralfaro, 1945, Madrid: Afrodisio Aguado, 1950).

Trampantojos (Buenos Aires: Colección "La cuerda floja," 1947).

Las tres gracias (Madrid: Editorial Perseo, 1949).

El turco de los nardos (Madrid: La Novela Actual, 1943).

Variaciones (Madrid: La Tribuna, 1920, 1925. Also, Madrid: Editorial Atenea, 1922, Madrid: Editorial La Nave, 1922).

Virguerías (Madrid: Author, 1920).

La viuda blanca y negra (Madrid: Biblioteca Nueva, 1917. Also, Buenos Aires: Editorial Poseidón, 1943).

SECONDARY SOURCES

ALFARO, MARIA, "Ante la muerte," *Indice de Artes y Letras* (Madrid), LXXVI (1955), 18. Studies abundant references to death in Ramón's works.

AMBRUZZI, LICIO, "Goya attraverso Ramón," *Convivium* (Torino), I (1929), 724-27. Notes similarity of spirit between Ramón and Goya, in their "Caprichos" and in Ramón's almost autobiographical biography of Goya.

AZNAR, JOSE RAMON, "Ramón en las cosas y en el arte," *Revista de Ideas estéticas* (Madrid), XXI (1963), 9-15. Helpful general observations on Ramón's style and subjective biographical writings.

BLEIBERG, GERMAN and JULIAN MARIAS, Editors. *Diccionario de literatura española (Madrid: Revista de Occidente, 1964)*. Excellent synthesis of Ramón's literary life, works, and style.

BORRAS, TOMAS, "El descubridor de continentes inéditos en el mar del castellano," *Revista de Ideas Estéticas* (Madrid), XXI (1963), 27-35. Insists that Ramón belongs to no period. Good insights into Ramón's use of language and humor, "things," biographical techniques, and the basic relationship between *greguerías* and metaphor.

———, "Los monigotes de Ramón," *La Estafeta Literaria* (Madrid), (January 19, 1963), p. 3. Comments on Ramón's sketches and doodles. Considers them indicative of his basically imagistic literary style.

CAMON AZNAR, JOSE, *Ramón Gómez de la Serna en sus obras* (Madrid: Espasa Calpe, S.A., 1972). The most extensive and intensive study of Ramón's works to date, an indispensable study despite its incomplete sentences and frequently subjective evaluations; includes partial résumés and valorative critiques of even little-known and hard-to-find works by Ramón.

CANO, JOSE LUIS, "Ramón Gómez de la Serna: *Las tres gracias,*" *Insula* (Madrid), IV, no. 45 (1949), 5. Perceptive review. Indicates that Madrid and its spirit (not the slim plot) is the basis of the novel.

———, "Ramón Gómez de la Serna: *Doña Juana la loca y otras novelas superhistóricas,*" *Insula* (Madrid), IV, no. 47 (1949), 5. Review. Opines that Ramón's creative poetic touch has added new life to the normally dull biographic genre.

CANSINOS ASSENS, RAFAEL, "Ramón Gómez de la Serna," *Poetas y prosistas del novecientos* (Madrid: Editorial América, 1919), 247-75. Traces antecedents of *greguería* in other writers. Stresses its graphic, caricaturesque qualities. Comments on Ramón's kaleidoscopic powers of observation and expression.

———, *La nueva literatura, IV: La evolución de la novela (1917-1927)* (Madrid: 1927), 351-83. Considers Ramón's Ultraist tendencies, notes fragmentary quality of his work, personification of things, graphic arbitrariness of style. This writer reiterates with slight modifications, his basic evaluation of Ramón in each of his studies on him.

CARDONA, RODOLFO, *Ramón, A study of Gómez de la Serna and His Works* (New York: Eliseo Torres and Sons, 1957). The best general study and critical analysis thus far available on Ramón's life, era, works, and literary style. Basically a revision of same writer's unpublished Ph. D. dissertation, "Ramón Gómez de la Serna; A Study of His Works and Personality," University of Washington, 1953.

CASTILLO PUCHE, J. L., "A la eternidad con monóculo," *Blanco y Negro* Madrid), num. 2646 (January 19, 1963), n.p. Necrological article. Considers Ramón's most valuable contribution to literature his new way of "seeing" things and plasticizing his insights verbally. Notes that his creative approach to biography achieved more complete presentations of subjects than traditional biographies.

CELA, CAMILO JOSE, "Ramón," *Papeles de Son Armadáns* (Madrid-Palma), VIII, Vol. 28, no. 83 (February, 1963), 115-18. Poetic necrological article describes Ramón as a martyr to literature, whose life and work were inseparably fused. Laments his illness, poverty, too-long delayed tangible proofs (awards, money) of recognition. Shows deep personal feeling for Ramón.

CERNUDA, LUIS, "Gómez de la Serna y la generación poética del 1925," *Estudios sobre poesía contemporánea* (Madrid: Ediciones Guadarrama, 1957), pp. 165-77. Stresses Ramón's poetic language and considers him the single most important influence on poets of the "Generation of 1925."

CHABAS, JUAN, "Ramón Gómez de la Serna," *Literatura española contemporánea (1898-1950)* (La Habana: Editorial Cultural, 1952), pp. 381-94. Balanced article includes negative criticism. Considers Ramón *madrileño*, rather than universal, profuse but inferior. Admits his influence on later writers. Evaluates his biographical works as subjective but successful.

DIEGO, GERARDO, *Lope y Ramón* (Madrid: Ateneo, 1963). Draws parallels between Ramón and Lope in personal exuberance and literary fecundity. Bases many of his ideas on the self-identification evident in Ramón's biographical study, *Lope viviente*.

ENTRAMBASAGUAS, JOAQUIN, "Ramón Gómez de la Serna," in *Las Mejores Novelas Contemporáneas* VIII (Barcelona: Editorial Planeta, 1957). Calls Ramón the "renovator and innovator" of Spanish contemporary literature. Stresses the importance of his influence on subsequent Spanish writers (especially poets). Lauds his *madrileñismo* and notes his attempts in areas of theater, children's tales, and biography. Excellent brief evaluations of a number of his novels.

ESPINA, ANTONIO, "Ramón, genio y figura," *Revista de Occidente*, 2nd period, I, no. 1 (1963), 54-64. Stresses Ramón's creative use of language, humor, poetry and *madrileñismo*. Considers his work a perfect example of Ortega's concept of "dehumanizing" art.

FERNANDEZ CUENCA, CARLOS, "En *El hombre perdido* plantea Ramón Gómez de la Serna la novela de la nebulosa y del azar," *Correo Literario* (Madrid), IV, num. 73 (1953), 16. Title is misleading. Excellent article quotes Ramón freely. Deals with his sacrifices to literature, problems with editors, nebulous novels, *Automoribundia*, and books on the Pombo.

FITZGERALD, THOMAS A., *"Azorín,* por Ramón Gómez de la Serna," *Hispania*, XIV (1931), 241-43. Excellent review. Considers Azorin a biography of "indirection," a mélange of the Madrid of '98 which succeeds in presenting an impressionistic portrait of Azorín.

GARCIA, FELIX, "En la cima de la vida," *ABC* (Madrid), (March 8, 1962), p. 1. Deals with Ramón's return to the practice of Catholicism.

GOMEZ DE LA SERNA, GASPAR, "Hacia el concepto de la greguería," *Papeles de Son Armadáns* (Mallorca), XXX (1963), 197-204. Believes the *greguería* achieves a graphic and poetic synthesis of expression and reveals planes of reality hidden to ordinary perception.

―――, *Ramón* (Madrid: Taurus, 1963). An indispensable biographical and literary study of Ramón. Includes the most comprehensive and penetrating criticism of his work to date. Many excerpts from Ramón's personal letters.

Selected Bibliography

GRANJEL, LUIS S., *Retrato de Ramón* (Madrid: Ediciones Guadarrama, 1963), n.p. A biography. Superficial compared with Gaspar Gómez de la Serna's more painstaking and penetrating study.

HORNEDO, RAFAEL MARIA, S. J., "El catolicismo de Ramón Gómez de la Serna," *Razón y Fe* (Madrid), CLXVII (1963), 344-56. Follows the trajectory of Catholicism in Ramón's life and works. Proves, through numerous examples of religious imagery that Ramón's religious *belief* continued even when his religious *practice* did not. Excerpts from Ramón's personal letters confirm his return to the practice of religion in his last years.

JACKSON, RICHARD LAWSON, "The Greguería of Ramón Gómez de la Serna: A Study of the Genesis, Composition, and Significance of a New Literary Genre," Unpublished Ph.D. dissertation, The Ohio State University, 1963. An in depth study of all aspects of the *greguería,* but particularly of its varying structures.

MARIAS, JULIAN, "Ramón y la realidad," *Insula* (Madrid), XII, no. 123 (February 15, 1957), 2, 8. Also in *El oficio del pensamiento* (Madrid: Revista de Occidente, 1958), 251-58. Believes that Ramón's passion for things saved him from being a realist, that he used reality as a basis for fantasy, decomposing and re-creating it.

MAZZETTI, RITA, "Some Comments on the Biographical Sketches of Ramón Gómez de la Serna," *Kentucky Romance Quarterly,* XVII, no. 4, 1970, 275-86. Analyzes the techniques of description, imitation, and anecdote used by Ramón in re-creating his biographical subjects.

――――, "Poetic Biography: A Study of the Biographical Works of Ramón Gómez de la Serna," Unpublished Ph.D. dissertation, Indiana University, 1968. After an introductory chapter on Ramón's literary life, the work is divided into two parts: The first is a study of Ramón's biographical works, the second is a stylistic analysis of the literary techniques discernible in these works.

――――, "The Use of Imagery in the Works of Ramón Gómez de la Serna," *Hispania,* LIV, no. 1 (March, 1971), 80-90. An intensive and systematic analysis of Ramón's use of imagery using diagrammatic patterns devised by the author.

MURCIANO, CARLOS, "La muerte, ese greguería," *Cuadernos Hispanoamericanos* (Madrid), LIII, no. 158 (1963), 297-99. Comments on *greguerías* concerning death.

――――, "La vida, esa greguería," *Punta Europa* (Madrid), no. 81 (1963), 24-36. Review of *Cartas a las golondrinas* with long series of excerpts; notes Ramón's predilection for images using cats, mirrors, and butterflies, and lists series of *greguerías* on each.

NORA, EUGENIO DE, "Ramón Gómez de la Serna," *La novela española contemporánea* (1927-1960) (Madrid: Editorial Gredos, Vol. II, I, 1962), 93-150. Concise summary of Ramón's life with brief summaries and criticism of some of his major novels. Too extensive for real depth, but helpful to those unfamiliar with Ramón and his work.

OBREGON, ANTONIO DE, "Cartas de Ramón," *ABC* (Madrid), (August 8, 1962), n.p. Through excerpts from Ramón's letters to Father Félix García, the author provides glimpses of the poverty, despair, and pathos of Ramón's declining years.

POLANCO BOTIN, ANTONIO, "La noche del sábado y el sábado sin noche," *Indice de Artes y Letras* (Madrid), LXXVI (1955), 14. Tells of the impossibility of reviving the Pombo *tertulia* during Ramón's return visit (1955) to Madrid, and gives a sentimental evocation of the Pombo of bygone days.

PONCE, FERNANDO, *Ramón Gómez de la Serna* (Madrid: Union Editorial, 1968). Wordy. Good for the reader who knows nothing of Ramón. To anyone who has read *Automoribundia,* or Gaspar Gómez de la Serna's *Ramón,* it seems a superficial summarizing of the two.

PORRAS, ANTONIO, "Los reaños del alma (Notas al *El Greco,* de Ramón Gómez de la Serna)," *Cruz y Raya* (Madrid), XXXII (1935), 137-44. A review of *El Greco.* Shows how Ramón re-creates the Spain of Greco's era. Notes Ramón's identification with his subject.

REYES, ALFONSO, "Ramón Gómez de la Serna," In *Simpatías y diferencias* (Mexico: Editorial Porrúa, 1945), pp. 68-79. Perceptive. Stresses the personalism of Ramón's style, its instinctive and emotional (rather than intellectual) qualities. A similar article by Reyes appears in *Tertulia de Madrid* (Buenos Aires: Espasa-Calpe Argentina, Colección Austral, 1949), pp. 95-106 and in *Hispania* (Paris), I, no. 3 (July, August, September, 1918), 234-40.

RIO, ANGEL DEL, "Miró y Gómez de la Serna," In *Historia de la literatura española II* (New York: Holt, Rinehart & Winston, 1963), pp. 317-26. Indicates that Ramón's work exemplifies Ortega's concept of "dehumanization" of art. Observes that humor, imagination, and "infrarealism" typify Ramón.

RIO, ANGEL DEL and BENARDETE, M. J., *El concepto contemporáneo de España: Antología de ensayos (1895-1931)* (Buenos Aires: Editorial Losada, 1946) p. 714-17. Considers Ramón a literary anarchist who violates unity and mixes all genres to arrive at pure humor and dehumanization.

ROSSI, HERNANI, "Comentarios al mejor libro del mes," *La Gaceta Literaria* (Madrid), V, num. 116 (October 1, 1931), 16. Believes that Gómez de la Serna made the metaphor essential to literature, brought forth a new kind of novel, not based on reality.

SALAVERRIA, JOSE MARIA "Un escritor," reprinted by Ramón Gómez de la Serna in *Libro nuevo,* pp. 33-36. (See primary sources.)

SALINAS, PEDRO, "Escorzo de Ramón," In *Literatura española siglo XX* (Mexico: Editorial Séneca, 1941), pp. 237-48. Emphasizes his blending of humor and pathos. Also comments on *Greguerías, Los muertos,* and *El rastro.*

SAMPELAYO, JUAN, "Ramón Gómez de la Serna: *Las tres gracias,*" *Escorial* (Madrid), 2nd period, XX, num. 60 (1949), 1280-81. Review. Considers the work more a chronicle of reminiscences or a sentimental poem on Madrid than a novel.

SENABRE SEMPERE, RICARDO, "Sobre la técnica de la greguería," *Papeles de Son Armadáns* (Mallorca), XLV, num. 134 (May, 1967), 121-45. Notes that the *greguería* reflects Ramón's attitude toward language.

SOFOVICH, LUISA, editor. *Diario póstumo de Ramón Gómez de la Serna* (Barcelona: Plaza y Janés, S. A., 1972). A carefully expurgated edition of Ramón's personal diary prepared for publication by Luisa Sofovich. A combination diary of brief recorded happenings and random thoughts.

TORRE, GUILLERMO DE, "Paralelismo entre Picasso y Ramón," *Insula* (Madrid), XVIII, num. 196 (1963), 1, 6. Also in *Síntesis* (Buenos Aires), I, num. 9 (January, 1928), 203-316. Compares the two in universality, fecundity, diversity. Parallels Ramón's *greguerías* with Picasso's Cubism, and affirms that both passed from periods of traditionalism to the abstract. A similar longer essay appears as a prologue to *Obras completas,* Volume II, by Ramón Gómez de la Serna, 1957. Also as "Picasso y Ramón," *Hispania,* XLV, no. 4 (December, 1962), 597-611.

TORRENTE BALLESTER, GONZALO, *Panorama de la literatura española contemporánea, I,* 2nd ed. (Madrid: Ediciones Guadarrama, 1961), pp. 276-81. Considers the *greguería* the basis of Ramón's style. Notes that in his search for novelty, Ramón created unusual novels and biographies.

———, "Teatro de Ramón," *Insula* (Madrid), XVIII, no. 196 (1963), 15. Considers Ramón's literary works and especially his theatrical pieces, as willfully capricious and based on the *greguería.*

VALENCIA, ANTONIO, *"Madrid, Ley de la novela de Ramón,"* *Arriba* (Madrid), (April 15, 1962), p. 23. Inspired by Ramón's *Piso bajo.* Claims that Ramón's inner core is Spanish and *madrileño,* that he knows or invents "facts" about Madrid which result in penetrating insights.

———, "El otro Ramón de América," *Arriba* (Madrid), (January 15, 1963), p. 23. Notes that in Ramón's literary production in America, biographical studies and intimate autobiographical works predominated, as he became more reflective and reminiscent.

YNDURAIN, FRANCISCO, "Sobre el arte de Ramón," *Revista de Ideas Estéticas* XXXI (1963), 37-45. Regrets that Ramón created no character or work which synthesized him, and believes that his value will be based more on what he attempted than on what he achieved.

SELECTED RELATED REFERENCES

ALONSO, DAMASO and CARLOS BOUSOÑO, *Seis calas en el estudio de la expresión literaria española* (Madrid: Editorial Gredos, 1963).

APOLLINAIRE, GUILLAUME, *Il y a . . . Poésies et prose inédites,* Preface by Ramón Gómez de la Serna (Paris: Albert Messein, 1925).

AZORIN (pseud. JOSE MARTINEZ RUIZ), *El artista y el estilo* (Madrid: Aguilar, 1946).

BOUSOÑO, CARLOS. *Teoría de la expresión poética* (Madrid: Editorial Gredos, 1956).

COROMINAS, JUAN. *Diccionario crítico etimológico de la lengua castellana*, II (Madrid: Editorial Gredos, 1954).

LOY, ROBERT J. "Things in Recent French Literature," *PMLA*, LXXI (March, 1965), 27-41.

ORTEGA Y GASSET, JOSÉ. *The Dehumanization of Art*. trans. William R. Trask (New York: Doubleday Anchor Books, 1956).

Index

The works of Gómez de la Serna are listed under his name.

Abril, Manuel, 99
Academie Goncourt, 112
Alfonso X, Grand Cross of, 34
Alonso, Dámaso: *Seis calas en el estudio de la expresión literaria,* 139
Ambient, novels of, 44-52
Amigos de Arte de Buenos Aires, 29
Amorós, Juan Bautista. *See* Lanza, Silverio
Anecdotal novels, 57-61
Argentina, 15, 29, 33, 34, 36, 60, 103, 108; Argentine Parliament, 35
Arriba, 32, 36, 37
Arsenic and Old Lace, 59
Ateneo of Madrid, 32, 91
Aurelius, Marcus, 29
Azorín (José Martínez Ruiz), 20, 21, 36, 44, 101-102, 106, 128, 142; *Doña Inés,* 20; *España,* 20; *Un pueblecito,* 20; See *also* Azorín

Bacarisse, Mauricio, 100
Baeza, Ricardo, 100
Barcelona, 28, 32, 111
Barney, Natalia, 106, 110
Baroja, Pío, 106, 111; *See also* "Pío Baroja"
Bartrina, Joaquín María, 109; *"Arabescos,"* 109; *"Intimas,"* 109
Baudelaire, Charles, 100, 131, 143; *See also* "El desgarrado Baudelaire"
Becquer, Gustavo Adolfo, 92; *Los ojos verdes,* 92
Benavente, Jacinto, 111, 119; *El príncipe que todo aprendió en los libros,* 111; *See also* "Benavente"
Blanchard, María Gutiérrez. See "María Gutiérrez Blanchard"
Blasco Ibañez, Vicente, 112; *See also* "Vicente Blasco Ibañez"
Bontempelli, Massimo, 107
Borges, Norah. See "Norah Borges"
Borrás, Tomás, 22, 34, 35
Busoño, Carlos: *Teoría de la expresión literaria,* 138-39
Bretón, Andre, 131; *Nadja,* 27
Bretón de los Herreros, Manuel, 35
Buenos Aires, 29, 30, 31, 32, 34, 35, 36, 44, 60, 89, 103, 122
Burgos, Carmen de, 19, 20, 99

Café des Vickings et de la Rotonde, 27
Calderón de la Barca, Pedro, 143
Calleja, Rafael, 135
Calvet, Romero, 99
Cami, 27, 107
Campoamor, Ramón de, 109; *Doloras,* 131; *Humoradas,* 131
Canelejas, José, 18
Cansinos Asséns, Rafael, 106, 111, 128, 131; *See also* "Cansinos Assens"
Cardona, Rodolfo, 19, 20, 27, 117, 135
Cardona, Peña, Alfredo, 104, 151n
Carrere, Emilio, 106, 107; *See also* "Emilio Carrere"
Cassou, Jean, 27, 106
Cernuda, Luis, 126, 132
Chabas, Juan, 141

[171]

Chagall, Mark. *See* "Marcos Chagall"
Chaplin, Charles, 117; Chaplinesque, 107; *see also* "Charlot"
Chekhov, Anton Pavlovich, 131
Civil War, 57, 103, 106
Cocteau, Jean, 102, 131; *"Serafismo,"* 102
Colette, (Willy), Sidonie Gabrielle, 17, 106, 128; *see also* "Colette"
Corominas, Juan, 130; *Diccionario de autoridades,* 130
Coronado, Carolina. *See Mi tía Carolina Coronado*

Dalí, Salvador, 36; *see also* "Daliísmo"
D'Annunzio, Gabriele, 21
Darío, Rubén, 131
d'Aurevilly, Barbey, 100
Delaunays, the: Robert and Sonia, 102
d'Ors, Eugenio, 99, 106, 110; *see also* "Eugenio d'Ors"

Echegaray, José, 112, 143; *see also* "Don José Echegaray"
Editors, 122, 123
Ehrenburg, Illya, 110
Españolismo, 48
Espronceda, José de, 35
Estoril, 23, 113

Falla, Manuel de. *See* "Manuel de Falla"
Fernández, Macedonio. *See* "Macedonio Fernández"
Fernández Almagro, Melchor, 105
Fichter, William L., 21
Florence, 18
Franco, Francisco, 32, 34
French Academy of Humor, 28, 107

Gallegos, Rómulo, 21
García Calderón, Ventura, 107-108
García Félix, 34, 35
García Luengo, Eusebio, 133
García Prieto, Manuel, 18
Gide, Andre, 17
Girondo, Oliverio, 30, 106, 107; *Espantapájaros,* 107; *see also,* "Oliverio Girondo"
God, 35, 115, 122, 124-25; *see also* "Dios"

Gómez de la Serna, Gaspar (cousin), 17, 33, 34, 112, 113, 132
Gómez de la Serna, Javier (father), 16, 17, 18, 23, 101
Gómez de la Serna, Julio (brother), 100
Gómez de la Serna, Ramón: childhood and adolescence, 15-17; paternal support, 17; Paris, 17-18; return to Madrid, 18; discovery of the *greguería,* 18-19; Carmen de Burgos, 19; early publications, dedication to a literary career, 19-20; establishes Pombo *tertulia,* 20-21; early periodical writing, 22-23; Ortega and the *Revista de Occidente,* 23-24; wanderings: Naples, 26; Paris, 27; Madrid, 27-28; Paris, 28; Berlin, 28; first attempt at theater, 28; first trip to Buenos Aires, meets Luisa Sofovich, 29; emigrates to Buenos Aires, 30-31; economic pressures, 31-32; return visit to Spain, 32; fiftieth anniversary, 33; literary awards, 34-35; illness and death, 35
WORKS:
"Abandonada en el Rastro, La," 88
"Adelantados, Los," 86
Alba, El, 18
*Antologí*a, 34
"Apestado, El," 92
"Aquella novela," 66
Automoribundia, 30, 31, 34, 35, 100, 112, 113-16, 117, 118
"Aventuras y desgracias de un sinsombrerista," 89
Azorín, 101-102, 103, 128, 134, 140, 142; *see also* Azorín
Bailarina, La, 40
"Bartrina", 109; *see also* Bartrina, Joaquín María
"Bazar más suntuoso del mundo," 93
Beatriz, 37
"Beltraneja, La," 86
"Benavente," 111, 134; *see also* Benavente, Jacinto
"Bernard Shaw," 109-110, 143; *see also,* Shaw, Bernard
Bontempelli y Pittigrilli, 107
"Botella y el candelabro, La," 94
"Botellismo," 102
"Brindis de los dos viudos," 98
"Caballero de Olmedo, El," 31, 84-85

Index

Caballero del hongo gris, El, 27
"Caja de Pandora, La," 92
"Cami," 107; *see also* Cami
"Cansinos Asséns," 111, 139; *see also* Cansinos Asséns, Rafael
Caprichos, 24
Cartas a las golondrinas, 32, 117
Cartas a mí mismo, 117-18
"Casa nueva, La," 38, 39
"Casa triangular, La," 71
"Cena de académicos," 94
Chalet de las rosas, El, 59
"Charlot," 134; *see also* Chaplin, Charles
"Ciego y la hetaira," 91-92
Cinelandia, 26, 59-60
Circo, El (The Circus), 19, 20; French translation, 26, 27
Cólera azul, El (Blue Cholera, Collection), 77-83
"El cólera azul," 77-78
"Colette," 109, 128; *see also* Colette (Willy), Sidonie Gabrielle
"Conde de Keyserling, El," 109
"Consignatarias, Las," 81
"Contra la pena," 97
Corona de hierro, 38-39
"Creador de los nacimientos, El," 95
Cuento de Callejo, 38, 111
Cuentos de fin de año, 90, 93-98
"Cuento de navidad con vidriera de colores," 96
Cuentos para los días de no salir de casa, 90
Cuentos para niños, 93
Cursi y otros ensayos, Lo, 36
"Dalíismo," 16
"Danza de los Apaches, La," 40
"Danza oriental, La," 40
"Danzas de la pasión, Las," 40
"De otra raza," 65
"Defensor del cementerio, El," 80
"Desgarrado Baudelaire, El," 134, 143
Desolación, 37
"Destrozonas" 80-81
"Dios," 115, 124-25; *see also* God
Disparates, 24, 105
Doctor inverosímil, El (The Unlikely Doctor) 26-27, 57-58; French translation, 26

Don Diego Velázquez, 31, 104, 127, 133, 139; *see also* Velázquez, Diego
"Don José Echegaray," 112
"Don Miguél de Unamuno," 109, 128, 130, 138; *see also* Unamuno, Miguel de
Don Ramón María del Valle-Inclán, 31, 105, 117, 130, 134, 139, 142, 143; *see also* Valle-Inclán, Ramón de
Doña Juana la loca (Collection), 31, 83-87
"Doña Juana la loca," 31, 83-84
"Doña Urraca de Castilla," 84
"Doncella, La," 92
"Dos espejos, Los," 40
"Dos marineros, Los," 67-68
Drama del palacio deshabitado, El, 37
Dueño del átomo, El (The Master of the Atom, Collection), 70-74
"Dueño del átomo, El," 70-71
Edgar Poe, genio de América, 29, 33, 115, 116, 128; *see also* Poe, Edgar Allen
"Editores, Los," 122, 123
Efigies (Effigies), 27, 29
"*Ella + Ella - El + El,* 81-82
"Emilia Pardo Bazán," 110
"Emilio Carrere," 107
"Emparedada de Burgos, La," 85-86
"Enrique Larreta," 108
Entrando en fuego, 17
"Epílogo," 98
Escaleras, Las, 40
"Esta noche en Rusia," 97
"Estufa de cristal, La," 79
"Eugenio d'Ors," 110
"Falta una copa," 97
Fiesta de Dolores, 40
"Francisco Vighi," 107; *see also* Vighi, Francisco
"Fuera de casa," 96
"Fúnebre, La," 68
"Gabán de nieve, El," 95
"Gabriel Miró," 109; *see also* Miró, Gabriel
"Gallipava, La," 64
"Gangosa, La," 65-66
"Gemelos y el guante, Los," 63
Gollerías, 24
Goya, 27, 100-101, 103, 117, 127; *see*

also Goya, Francisco
"Gran griposo, El," 72
Gran hotel, El, 58
"Gravedad e importancia del humorismo," 17
Greco, El, 29, 102-103, 115, 136; *see also* Greco, El
Greguerías, 19, 29, 100, 129; *see also* Greguerías
Greguerías completas, 34
"Hidalgo y el maquinista, El," 96
"Hija del verano, La," 72
"Hijo del millonario, El," 70
"Hijo surrealista, El," 88-89
Hiperestésica, La (Collection), 74-77
"Hiperestésica, La," 74-75
"Hombre de la galería, El," 72-73
"Hombre de los pies grandes, El," 74
Hombre perdido, El, (The Lost Man), 25, 29, 43, 55-56
"Ibsen," 108, 109
"Ildefonso Cuadrado," 98
Incongruente, El (The Incongruent One), 26, 27, 31, 43, 53-54, 115; French translation, 26
Ismos, 102, 106
"Jazzbandismo," 102
José Gutiérrez Solana, 31, 104, 117; *see also* Solana, José Gutiérrez
"José Pijoan," 110
"Joven de los sobremesas, El," 63-64
"Juan Ramón Jiménez," 110, 133, 143; *see also* Jiménez, Juan Ramón
"Kafka," 108, 109, 128, 142; *see also* Kafka, Franz
"Klaxismo," 102
"Laberinto, El," 38
"Leopoldo y Teresa," 87-88
Lope de Vega, 104; *see also* Vega, Lope de
Lope viviente, 31, 33, 104, 113, 138
"Luis Ruiz Contreras," 111; *see also* Ruiz Contreras, Luis
"Lunático, El," 38
"Mac-Orlan," 107-108
"Macedonio Fernández," 108, 109
Madrid, 101
Malicia de las acacias, La (The Malice of the Acacia Flowers, Collection), 62-66
"Malicia de las acacias, La," 62-63

"Manuel de Falla," 109
"Marcos Chagall," 136
"María Yarsilovna," 67
"María Gutiérrez Blanchard," 128
"Marquesito en el circo, El," 93
"Maruja Mallo," 31, 104, 127, 137
Medios seres, Los, 28, 39-40
Mi tía Carolina Coronado, 31, 104
"Miedo al mar," 65
Morbideces (Collection), 90-93
"Morbideces," 91
"Muerte del lunático, La," 92
Muertos y las muertas, Los, 29
Muestrarios, 24
Mujer de ambar, La (The Amber Woman), 27, 43, 44, 47-48, 51
"Mujer vestido de hombre, La," 69
Nardo, La (The Spikenard), 29, 43, 44, 45, 49-51, 52
"Natalicio del poeta, El," 95
"Niña Alcira, La," 79-80
"Nochebuena del año dos mil quinientos," 94
"Norah Borges," 104
Nostalgias de Madrid, 33
Novelista, El, 26, 54-55
Nuevas páginas de mi vida, (New Pages of My Life), 111, 117-19
Nuevo amor, El, 40
Nuevos retratos contemporáneos (New Contemporary Portraits), 31, 106, 109, 111,
Obras completas, 41
"Oliverio Girondo," 107; *see also* Girondo, Oliverio
"Olor de las mimosas, El," 73-74
"Olvido," 93-94
"Oscar Wilde," 130, 132, 143; *see also* Wilde, Oscar
Otras fantasmagorías, 29
Otros bailes, Los, 40-41
"Pablo Neruda," 109, 127; *see also* Neruda, Pablo
"Pablo Picasso," 130; *see also* Picasso, Pablo
Páginas escogidas e inéditas de Silverio Lanza (ed. and prologue), 20
"Palabras y lo indecible, Las," 135
Palacio deshabitado, El, 37
"Pandero de Rosaura, El," 95
"Paul Morand," 108; *see also*

Index

Morand, Paul
"Pedro de Répide," 109, 134; *see also* Répide, Pedro de
"Peluquería feliz," 78-79
"Pérez Galdós," *see* Pérez Galdós, Benito
"Perspectivas de España," 123-24
"Pío Baroja." *See* Baroja, Pío
Piso bajo, 44, 52
"Pirandello," 143
Policéfalo y señora, 60-61
Pombo, 22, 99, 100, 106, 107, 111, 129; *see also* Pombo
"Por los tejados," 93
Prado, El, 101; *see also* Prado, El
"Pueblo de Morenas," 82-83
Quevedo, 29, 33, 115, 116, 134, 138, 142, 143; *see also* Quevedo, Francisco
Quinta de Palmyra, La (Palmyra's Country Villa), 26, 43, 47
Ramonismo, 24-25
Rastro, El (The Flea Market), 20, 21, 22, 101, 107; *see also* Rastro, el
¡*Rebeca!*, 31, 43, 56-57
"Regalo del doctor, El," 75-76
"Remy de Gourmont," 109, 143; *see also* Gourmont, Remy de
"Retrato del Conde Villiers de l'Isle-Adam." *See* Villiers
Retratos contemporáneos (Contemporary Portraits), 31, 106, 111, 112, 129
"Roja, La," 76
Rosas rojas, Las, 40
"Ruso, El," 71-72
Sagrado cripto de Pombo, La, 99, 111
"Saint-Paul Roux," 109
"Saturada, La," 73
"Se presentó el hígado," 81
Secreto del acueducto, El (The Secret of the Aqueduct), 24, 46-47, 51
Seis falsas novelas (Six Pseudo Novels, Collection), 66-70
Senos, 19, 20; French translation, 26
Siempreviva, 38
"Siete Infantes de Lara, Los," 31, 86-87
"Sin estar yo," 98
Sonámbulos, Los, 38
"Suicida Gerardo de Nerval, El," 134, 141; *see also* Nerval, Gerardo de
"Suspensión del destino," 80
Teatro en soledad, 39
"Tía Marta, La," 94-95
"Toda la historia de la Calle de Alcalá," 101
"Toda la historia de la Plaza Mayor," 101
Toda la historia de la Puerta de Sol, 101
Torero Caracho, El (Caracho, the Toreador), 26, 29, 44, 48-49
"Tormenta, La," 64
Trampantojos, 24
Tránsito, 38
Tres gracias, Las (The Three Graces), 32, 44, 51-52
"Turco de las nardos, El," 89-90
Unánimes, Los, 38
Utopía, La, 37
Variaciones, 24
"Vegetariano, El," 76-77
"Viejo de las barbas de algodón, El," 96
"Virgen pintada de rojo, La," 68-69
Virguerías, 24
Viuda blanca y negra, La, 19, 45-46, 51; French translation, 26
Góngora, Luis de Argote y, 126, 138, 143
González Martínez, Enrique, 21
Gourmont, Remy de 18, 100, 106, 109, 143; *Une nuit au Luxembourg*, 18; *see also* "Remy de Gourmont"
Goya, Francisco, 16, 36, 100, 101, 104, 114, 127, 133, 137; *Caprichos*, 101; *see also* Goya
Greco, El, 16, 102, 103; *see also* El Greco
Greguerías, 18-19, 34, 35, 41, 42, 44, 55, 101, 115, 116, 128, 130-35
Guzmán, Martín Luís, 21

Henríquez Ureña, Pedro, 21
Holmes, Sherlock, 57
Horace, 131
Hornedo, Rafael María, 129
Hoyos, Antonio de, 106
Humor, 15, 16-17, 20, 29, 49, 59, 102, 107, 114, 115, 116-17, 118
Huxley, Aldus, 23

Jacob, Max, 27
Jiménez, Juan Ramón, 17, 110, 143;

Platero y yo, 110; *see also* "Juan Ramón Jiménez"
Juan Palomo Award, 34
Jung, Karl Gustav, 23

Kafka, Franz, 23, 53, 108, 109, 142
Keyserling, Count Hermann, 23, 109; *see also,* "El Conde de Keyserling"
Khayam, Omar, 29
Krausism, 23

Lanza, Silverio, 20, 34; *Páginas escogidas e inéditas de Silverio Lanza,* 20
Larbaud, Valery, 17, 27
Larra, Mariano José de, 20, 35, 52
Larreta, Enrique. *See* "Enrique Larreta"
Laurencin, Marie, 102
Lawrence, D. H. 23
liberal, El, 22, 23, 36
Lipchitz, Jaques, 21, 22
Llhote, 102
Lorca, Frederico García, 131
Lucian, 131
Luxembourg Gardens, 18, 66

Mac-Orlan, Pierre. *See* "Mac-Orlan"
Madrid, 15, 18, 20, 21, 22, 26, 27, 28, 29, 30, 32, 33, 34, 35, 36, 44, 45, 46, 48, 49, 50, 51, 52, 58, 65, 88, 91, 92, 104, 109, 127, 129; City Council of, 35
Mallo, Maruja. *See* "Maruja Mallo"
Maortua, Carlos, 30
Marías, Julián, 21-22, 24
Massa, Pedro, 153, Chapter Six, n. 2, 3, 4
Mesa, Enrique de, 108
Mesoneros Romanos, Ramón de, 52
Metaphor, 126-27, 128, 131
Miró, Gabriel, 17; *see also* "Gabriel Miró"
Morand, Paul, 106, 108; *see also* "Paul Morand"
Murciano, Carlos, 128

Naples, 26, 43, 44, 45, 47-48, 49, 72
Nación, La, 26, 30
Nebulous novels, 52-57
Neruda, Pablo, 21, 109, 127

Nerval, Gerardo de, 18, 29, 100; *see also* "El suicida Gerardo de Nerval"
Nobel Prize, 33, 112
Noel, Eugenio, 107-108

Ortega y Gasset, José, 22, 23, 24, 28, 36, 103, 106, 122
Ovid, 131

P.E.N. Club (International Association of Poets, Playwrights, Editors, Essayists and Novelists), 30
Panteón de Hombres Ilustres, 35
Papini, Giovanni, 21
Pardo Bazán, Emilia. *See* "Emilia Pardo Bazán"
Paris, 15, 17, 18, 22, 27, 28, 44, 45, 46, 50, 54, 60, 71, 72, 76, 78, 96, 100, 107
Pascal, Blaise, 29
Pérez Galdos, Benito, 50, 11; *Episodios nacionales,* 111
Perón, Juan, 34
Personification, 129
Picasso, Pablo, 24, 36, 102, 130; *see also* "Pablo Picasso"
Pijoán, José. *See* "José Pijoán"
Pitigrilli, Dino Segri, 107
Poe, Edgar Allen, 32, 117, 128, 143; *see also Edgar Poe, genio de América*
Pombo, 20-21, 22, 27, 28, 30, 99, 104, 107; *see also Pombo*
Portugal, 44, 47, 49
Prado, El, 16, 101; *see also El Prado*
Premio March (March Award), 34, 35
Primo de Rivera, Miguel, 23, 28
Prometeo, 17, 37, 40, 62, 99
Proust, Marcel, 17
Pyrrhus, 29

Quevedo, Francisco, 32, 36, 116, 117, 141, 142, 143; *see also Quevedo*

Rastro, El (Flea Market), 21, 45, 50, 80, 88, 102, 119; *see also El Rastro*
Religious images, 128-29
Répide, Pedro de, 109; *see also* "Pedro de Répide"
Revista de Occidente, 23, 24, 36, 37, 62
Reyes, Alfonso, 21
Río, Angel del, 129

Index

Rimbaud, Arthur, 131
Rivera, Diego, 22, 102
Rocamora, Pedro, 32
Rossi, Herani, 126
Roux, Saint-Paul. *See* "Saint-Paul Roux"
Ruiz Contreras, Luis, 106, 111
Ruskin, John, 19, 99, 100; *Stones of Venice*, 19, 99

Sainz de Robles, Federico, 24
Salaverría, José María, 130, 140, 141-42
Salinas, Pedro, 132
Sawa, Alejandro, 20
Senabre Sempere, Ricardo, 135-36
Seneca, 29
Shattuck, Roger, 17
Shaw, George Bernard, 109-110, 143
Schopenhauer, Arthur, 29
Sofovich, Luisa, 29, 30-31, 35, 89, 103
Sol, El, 22, 23, 26, 28, 36, 63
Solana, José Gutiérrez, 21, 104, 114; *see also José Gutiérrez Solana*
Spanish Academy (Real Academia de la lengua), 111
Spain, 22, 26, 28, 29, 30, 32, 33, 34, 36, 76, 103, 104, 106, 110, 113, 116, 122, 123-24, 127, 128, 135
Spengler, Oswald, 23
Staël, Madame, 133
Superhistorical novels, 83-87
Surrealism, 43, 128

Tarr, F. Courtney, 21
Tertulia (s), 21-22, 27, 28, 30, 99, 104, 111
Torre, Guillermo de, 135

Torrente Ballester, Gonzalo, 141
Torreón, 23
Torres Bodet, Jaime, 21
Tribuna, La, 18, 22, 36, 101
Tzara, Tristán, 21

Ultraist movement, 111; *see also* Cansinos Asséns, Rafael
Unamuno, Miguel de, 33, 106, 109, 122, 128, 143; *see also* "Don Miguel de Unamuno"

Valencia, Antonio, 32
Valle-Inclán, Ramón de, 20, 36, 105-106, 142, 143; *Esperpentos,* 105, 142; *see also Don Ramón María del Valle-Inclán*
Velázquez, Diego, 16, 127; *see also Don Diego Velázquez*
Ventanal, El, 23, 26
Vega, Lope de, 36, 104, 113, 143; *see also Lope de Vega, Lope viviente*
Vighi, Francisco, 106, 107; *see also* "Francisco Vighi"
Villalón, Fernando, 107
Villiers de, l'Isle-Adam, 100
Vossler, Karl, 21
Voz, La, 22

Wilde, Oscar, 99, 100, 113, 131, 132, 143, 144; *The Importance of Being Ernest,* 144; *see also* "Oscar Wilde"
World War I, 17, 22

Ynduraín, Francisco, 135

Zorrilla, José, 131